The F.A.C.E

of

Leadership

Jaymie V Pottinger

Acknowledgement

The ping on my phone alerted me to a new text message from my wife-Chauna. The message was a picture of me on what appeared as the title of a book that read *The FACE of Leadership*. She took the time out to design a book cover when this book was just an idea. This was her way of telling me to get up and start writing my book. It was a well-placed nudge and now here we are.

None of this would be possible without my God and Savior Jesus Christ. His wisdom and guidance have been the foundation of my life. His manifold blessings towards me manifested in the many amazing people He's strategically placed in my life to guide and establish my journey. Before being a leader of any organization, one must master leadership at home.

I can't say I've always scored an "A" in this department but my perspective on leadership has been impacted a great deal by my family. The publication of this book would not be possible without the unwavering support of my wife-Chauna. Thank you for all the love and support in making this possible. To my beautiful princesses Je`Chaun and Jenna and my prince Jaymie II, thank you for enriching my life with your affection, brilliance, and candor.

To my parents, Timothy, and Prudence Pottinger your relentless love, support and belief in my abilities has served as a source of inspiration and direction for my path. Thank you for your investment in me, I hope I've made good on the returns. To all my siblings Josann, Jermane, Judy-Ann, Jannine, Joni Dean, Jenille and Jevaughn I love you. I am the man I am today because each of you have poured love and confidence into me.

A very special word of gratitude to my fellow citizens of Labyrinth. Your words of affirmation and kindness has shaped my early development in a very positive way. To my childhood friends and family: Uncle Sulton, Lamar, Masai, Tony, Marshall, Lamar, Tentae, Jason, Latty, and Dwayne, thank you.

I've had the utmost privilege to be surrounded by a village of supporters. Patrice Williams-Gordon, Luigi Allen, Noel Reid, Dwayne Mars, Robert Miller, Ryan Wiggan, Sherlon Leon, Delmas Campbell, Kris Fielder, Lawrance Martin, Nicole Hughes, Russell Patterson, Dr. Glen Baker and Yvette Weir have been a pillar of support along my journey. Your love and encouragement means the world to me.

Very special shout out to my friends and supporters: Black at Microsoft (BAM) Dallas and Costa Rica. Before *The FACE of Leadership* was published, you invested, and I am eternally grateful. Thank you!

Foreword

Leadership is the nucleus of institutions. The nucleus of a cell contains information that directs the functions of that small but complex system. The nucleus directs nutrients to the right places for building new structures or replacing old ones. It also communicates with other nuclei in neighboring cells to ensure that the larger body to which they belong, can carry out similar functions on a larger scale. Accurate information in the nucleus is vital to the integrity and reproduction of the cell. Loss of information in the nucleus leads to breakdown and dissolution of the cell. In some cases, corrupted information leads to corrupted reproduction. We call this cancer.

In similar fashion, leadership in human institutions must execute a cluster of vital functions. Typical institutions include those in education and medicine in both the public and charitable sectors. They also include business enterprises, church administrations, and government departments. Leaders must provide the vision, inspiration, delegation, negotiation, inspection, and conflict-resolution that enable the institution to carry out its mission, reproduce itself, and coordinate with other institutions for the greater good of the larger economy and culture.

This book by Jaymie Pottinger offers some essential elements of the DNA that inform healthy functioning. It will be useful to existing and aspiring leaders of all kinds of institutions. Pottinger's gene sequence is coded in the acronym F.A.C.E. It evokes a double-helix in the sense that each letter in the acronym occurs twice. This coding organizes the notional and practical guidance for leadership at any level.

These insights on effective leadership derive from both inspiration and experience. As a man of faith and reflection, Pottinger spent years in deepening the wisdom that comes from knowing God. As an experienced teacher, coach, Dean of students, and educational administrator, he has developed and refined effective strategies of leadership. Projects that failed provided lessons. Those that worked were reproduced and adapted for changing environments. The book is a product of the process.

Effective institutional leaders are urgently needed because contemporary threats to the larger economy are increasing. These include widening inequality, violent conflict, and environmental deterioration. Local leadership can make significant contributions in addressing these problems.

Threats to the larger culture are also increasing. Disregard for truth, selfish individualism, racism, and other forms of intolerance all undermine solidarity. The world therefore needs leaders of economy and society who will FACE the demands of truth, equity, and social cohesion.

This contribution by Jaymie Pottinger is a welcome addition to the prescriptions for shrinking the cancers of society, and for promoting the optimal health of economy and culture. Large visions are realized by practical steps of the kind that Pottinger describes.

Michael H. Allen, Ph.D.
Bryn Mawr College, Pennsylvania

Contents

Chapter One:
The F.A.C.E.

I used my tiny eight-year-old frame to block the doorway as I stood in the verandah of the place I called home, situated in a quiet farming community called Labyrinth-Jamaica. In today's edition of make-believe, our house was no longer a house, it was a school—my school. I was not Jaymie, The Big Brother anymore. I was Jaymie, The School Principal. My sisters, Sasha, and Joni, were parents to our barely toddler siblings, Breezie and Jev.

With my hands akimbo, my feet firmly planted on the red oak-stained floor, my intense aura exuded the authority of one who has been doing this job for years. I could not have felt more at home. It felt like my true passion and calling.

They had to submit to a very thorough inspection before any of them could get by me. Quite often, their standards of attire fell short of the established ethos of my institution, which gave me no choice but to put my foot down and show them who was in charge.

"I cannot allow you into my school when you look like this. Go home and ask your mother to wash your face," were the words that would often descend from my lips at the sight of these untidy pupils.

While some aspects of these stories elude me, and the finer details consistently escape my recollection, I am never short of reminders. Although I am not the eldest of all my siblings, my affinity for leadership was evident from a tender age. In several of their conversations with my friends, my siblings often (at my expense) share tales of my leadership from when I was merely a child.

There has been a long-standing debate within the business arena over whether leaders are born or created. As a student of leadership, I often find myself amidst such fiery discussions. In this book, however, I will resist the urge to engage in this debate. Instead, I will answer some of the most complex questions regarding leadership and its effectiveness—a standard that I believe is achievable but often overlooked.

From personal experience and the extensive research I've conducted, I take no hesitation in asserting an undeniable fact; whether you were born a leader, or you accidentally stumbled into a position that requires leadership, whether you are new to leadership or seasoned and experienced, whether you are leading yourself, a team or an organization, leadership development is an absolute necessity. Leadership development decides the fate of your legacy as a leader. A true leader needs the FACE of Leadership in their arsenal.

The true role of a leader has been explained in a straightforward statement, 'to produce great results.' While this essential factor is clear, the one area that consistently eludes both seasoned and aspiring leaders is how to attain these results.

While it is true that we may never be able to point to a single personality trait, gender, or profile that fully captures the FACE of an effective leader, we believe that the principles of the FACE of Leadership will have a transformative effect on any individual, team, or organization, regardless of their personality, gender, creed, or profile.

Have you ever missed an opportunity to lend your voice and wisdom to a decision-making process that could have revolutionized your team and organization? Or have you ever felt the disappointment of being overlooked for a promotion? Are you that person who has experienced difficulty articulating your ideas and thoughts on a given subject that would help your team realize their goals? Are you a recently promoted team leader struggling to bring the members of your team to work in a cohesive way?

The FACE of Leadership is a proven system that will help you break through these barriers and bring you closer to your personal and professional goals as a leader.

Whether you are new to leadership, or it is an aspirational goal on your vision board—this system will be a game-changer for you. When fully engaged, the eight elements of the FACE put forth in this book will position you as an assertive and decisive force within the leadership landscape.

I have spent the better part of the past 16 years engaged in thorough research pertaining to the habits, behaviors, and practices of some of the most influential leaders who have influenced change on a global scale.

As an executive and personal development coach, experience and observations have helped me uncover the secret sauce to the recipe for success as a contemporary leader. I have had the profound privilege of interviewing leaders whose successes have been declared to be exceptional.

Each of the leaders studied demonstrated that they have incorporated to a high degree, and managed very well the following elements highlighted within the FACE framework as part of their leadership strategy: Failure, Foresight, Awareness, Agility, Confidence, Clarity, Energy, and Execution.

When you deepen your understanding of each of these power-packed elements and their applicability to your leadership style, you develop the ability to influence your team, your superiors, and key stakeholders in a way that will place you in a completely different lane—an Exceptional Leader.

In this book, each chapter explicates one of the eight principles, providing you with a detailed breakdown of how each of them can be implemented as you navigate your way through challenges along your leadership journey.

The leadership arena has been abuzz with words like vulnerability, agility, grit, resilience, and diversity. These words have stimulated discussion among contemporary scholars about what drives organizational excellence and high-performance teams.

Today's leaders face a multiplicity of challenges that will inevitably outweigh their natural leadership abilities at times. The leader of the day must be prepared to answer the increasing calls for fostering a culture that inspires and builds responsive and cohesive teams, whether they lead teams that are 100% in-person, virtual or hybrid. While doing this, they must equally ensure that shareholders are satisfied, as reflected in quarterly reviews of the key performance metrics.

The leaders who will successfully meet the moment and deliver superior results will:

1. Embrace failure as an opportunity to learn and put in place response measures to insulate them from its paralyzing effects on their overall growth and development. **(Failure)**

2. Effectively anticipate and plan for future uncertainties with a sense of urgency and intentionality to future-proof their career, teams, and organization from the mounting challenges ahead. **(Foresight)**

3. Seek and develop an awareness of who they are as a leader, in terms of their own strengths and weaknesses, thereby leveraging their strengths while limiting the impact of their potential blind spots in realizing goals, building influence, and

being a catalyst for positive change. **(Awareness)**

4. Implement the key tenets of agility as part of their leadership approach to ensure they remain on the cutting edge to inspire growth and sustain excellence in the areas of service delivery, customer satisfaction, and innovation. **(Agility)**

5. Exude the confidence necessary to push through regardless of the challenges they face and inspire their team to commit to the vision of their organization. **(Confidence)**

6. Seek, obtain, and provide clarity on the work to be done, how it should be done as well as who should get it done. **(Clarity)**

7. Recognize the role of leadership energy in inspiring confidence in others around them. A leader should bring the energy every single time, recognizing they are the ones who will set the temperature in the room. **(Energy)**

8. Build a strong legacy through the vehicle of execution. They will learn how to prioritize what is essential and take the necessary steps to get things done. **(Execution)**

A leader, who lacks the ability to activate these eight principles as part of their overall growth and development, will struggle with being overlooked or perceived as incompetent by their team. And if they were naturally endowed with certain leadership capabilities, they would not secure the respect of their colleagues or team to stimulate organizational growth. The FACE of Leadership is what will take you to the next level of your career.

We will explore some of the key strategies to help you incorporate the principles of FACE on your leadership journey, as well as the consequences that may arise from not following these principles. Furthermore, we will provide some compelling examples of how using each of these principles has shaped the course of history.

Chapter Two:
Failure

"I know I will eventually fail, and I'm still all in. I've never met a brave person who hasn't known disappointment, failure, even heartbreak."
—Brene` Brown[i]

It is undoubtedly off-putting to talk about failure at the beginning of a book sub-titled *'How to Become a Strong and Effective Leader.'* But in reality, no one becomes a great leader without failing at some point. With great position comes great risk, and an effective leader is one who is well-informed on the skills and techniques of combatting and managing failure and using it as a power tool instead of allowing it to become a hindrance.

If there existed a checklist of characteristics for an effective leader, resilience would certainly be at the top. A smooth journey without any obstacles and challenges cannot produce an effective leader. Resilience not only teaches an individual to persevere in the face of adversity. It also gives us the grit to manage failure and come through on the other end, stronger and more prepared for the road ahead..

Unwittingly, we've allowed ourselves to be overtaken by the misguided notion that great leaders spend most of their time succeeding at what they do. We see them raise their glasses, throw parties, and beam with pride at the successes yielded from investing the time and work necessary to produce great results.

Looking from the outside, they all seem to be great at one thing: winning. It gives rise to the notion that a great leader is one who is always succeeding. Unfortunately, the picture-perfect scenario presented to us by the media has idolized success while demonizing failure. The truth is quite the opposite; all successes result from failures and trials.

The general perception of failure has been shaped through culture as a negative thing that should be avoided at all costs. However, even with the best of strategies in place, we run the risk of failing. Possessing the resilience to surmount these experiences will bring about some of the most exhilarating moments of your leadership journey.

In this book, our aim is not to romanticize failure; but instead to convince you to shift your paradigm on the role that failure plays in a successful journey. My goal is to change the prevalent perception of failure and help you see failure as a more natural part of the process, so it won't be as scary as it was before.

There are certain types of failures that can strike a fatal blow to one's reputation as a leader. In such cases, learning from other people's mistakes is a healthy alternative to having an experience of your own. It is critical to understand the difference between failures and abortive actions. Acts such as fraud, money laundering, or other unethical and criminal behaviors are the outcomes of this type of failure, and as we go about our journey, we must at all costs avoid these moral traps.

While conducting research for this book, I learned a great deal about habits, principles, and behaviors that drive the stellar achievements of great leaders. When we take a closer look into the conduct of these successful leaders, it becomes evident that they, too, have faced some monumental failures.

It would not be an overstatement to say that most leaders have created their best work as artists, writers, civil rights activists, speakers, runners, singers, and warriors by applying the lessons learned from failures.

On the road to success, failure is inevitable. Call it a rite of passage if you will. Every person fails at something, and if you have not yet failed at anything, you have either not been brave enough to pursue your calling, or you are on the verge of coming face-to-face with failure. If you are seeking something of significance, you must brace yourself for bumping into failure at some point along the way.

My intention is not to sentimentalize failure as something attractive. Indeed, failure leaves a very unpleasant after-taste. However, the consequences of failure are only prevalent amongst those who fail to remain vigilant during these 'un-successes,' for it can have a paralyzing effect on your overall growth. Failure puts every single fiber of our resilience to the test.

Depending on the severity and frequency of the failures we experience, we are certain to begin second-guessing our abilities and motives. Failure is deflating which in turn causes you to question your purpose.

Some leaders spiritualize failure, which is a cop-out(in my opinion). They feel that their failure is a sign from God that they are engaged in something wrong or that they are overly ambitious. As a result, they return to mediocrity, squandering an incredible opportunity to realize their God-given potential.

Since they require an excuse to quit, some leaders would see failure as an answer to their prayer. Failure tends to exaggerate our flaws, highlighting that we are not invincible and that achieving great goals will require more than our innate strength. As we consider the *Face of Leadership*, we must come to terms with the idea that there is no easy path to great achievement.

Levels to Failure

As Leaders, we may anticipate failure at multiple levels. The first degree of failure is personal failure, which has a significant impact on our life, growth, opportunities, and reputation but is not felt by others.

The next degree of failure is team failure, which affects the entire team as well as the organization. Since the leader is the ultimate decision-maker, they are often held accountable for the misfiring of the plans and the un-successes. Having experienced failure on both degrees, I'd like to think I can handle personal failure more efficiently than failure that affects my entire team.

While coaching a varsity soccer team, my team and I went the extra mile to prepare for the next season. We spent the entire pre-season working on drills and strategies, bonding as a team, and strategizing how to dominate the league. It was now time for our first friendly game, and we were beaming with excitement since we were convinced (based on the effort and time we had put into our preparations) that it would be a breeze.

However, our team was in for a rude awakening. We were behind 4:0 within the first twenty minutes of our first game. It was devastating! Some of the players had requested that they be removed from the game because nothing we had practiced seemed to be working. I began to doubt my ability to lead the team. By the end of the game, we were behind seven goals.

That evening, we walked back to our bus feeling like failures. On our walk back to the bus, I attempted to motivate the players, but I could see their faces scarred with disappointment and failure. I later learned that the goalkeeper was going to quit the team for the remainder of the season. Things were falling apart rapidly.

I went home that evening with the realization that I had failed the entire squad. As a coach, I was unable to deliver the promised victory. I spent some time reflecting on the game and gathered myself. The next day, I met with the players and told them that we could either use the loss as motivation to improve or take it as a sign that we are bad and forfeit all our forthcoming games.

I am unsure whether the students realized that I was

taking the team's loss too personally. Nonetheless, I recall one of the players stating in clear disagreement, "We all lost, and it is up to us to get back on the field together and win."

The gentle rebuke from this student was not lost on me. I shared with the players that we were slated to go up against the same team in another month, and perhaps, we could use the impending re-match as a gauge of our progress.

While we did not emerge as the victors against the team in our re-match, we were able to finish the game 2:1, which was a significant improvement over our first encounter, and it felt like a victory.

A team that had been humiliated at the start of the season rose to the occasion in a re-match and bravely competed. It was a wonderful spectacle, despite the pain of loss.

The team put up a similar fight throughout the remainder of the season. They did not let defeat or failure define them. Instead, they manipulated the challenges to propel them forward.

After suffering an embarrassing defeat at the beginning of the season, I must admit that I was deflated. However, I was reminded that the failure must be assessed, and the outcomes are utilized to plan the route ahead.

As the team's leader and coach, it was essential to

maintain my enthusiasm and confidence in the face of failure and disappointment. Even if the only thing to feel confident in was the hope of fighting another day, this confidence was required. As a leader, it was my responsibility to reassure the team that it wasn't the end of the world and that we still had it in us to achieve better.

Taking a team loss too personally can cripple our ability to inspire and encourage others to move past the sting of defeat. Always remember, when working on a team, the team's success should always take precedence over personal success.

On days like this, the words of Sir Winston Churchill[ii] ring true: "Success is not final, failure is not fatal, it is the courage to continue that counts." It may seem easier to give up when faced with defeat or difficult conditions, but it is critical to find the courage, grit, and resilience to rise above our failures—stronger and more prepared for the next climb.

My team defied the odds stacked against them, and I couldn't be prouder. This one experience prepared us well for the season ahead. We confronted and assessed all other games we lost head-on, which allowed us to confidently meet new challenges and emerge as the top team for our division that season.

Leaders Who Overcame Failure:
Thomas Edison and Abraham Lincoln

Failure does not discriminate and plays a starring role in everyone's story—regardless of race, creed, or culture. Many take it as a sign to throw in the towel or wave the white flag in surrender and move on to something new.

The problem lies with the mentality, as many of us regard failure as a dead-end, with no escape route? We have allowed failure to be the final decision-maker on the fate of our leadership and success journey. Should we be afraid of failure, or should we embrace it as a learning opportunity that will lead us to success?

In the January of 1879, Thomas Edison had built his first high resistance, incandescent electric light at his laboratory in Menlo Park, New Jersey. After multiple failed attempts, Edison, who would later be regarded by the world as the inventor of the light bulb, said, "I have not failed. I've just found 10,000 ways that won't work... many of the failures experienced are by people who did not realize how close they were to success when they gave up.[iii]"

For a man who had been expelled from his institution and called slurs such as 'abnormal' and a 'failure,' it certainly must have taken every ounce of his being to remain confident in himself. If Thomas Edison could treat his first encounter with failure as a lesson and a natural part of his success journey, what is stopping you from doing the same? This man, who both literally and figuratively enlightened our darkened homes through his invention, could never have made such a tremendous discovery had he not embraced his failures.

Although you may argue that Thomas Edison was not necessarily a leader, his influence is still felt today and deserves recognition. However, there is another figure who was a leader in the true sense of the word and had experienced failures both on personal and collective levels. He is one of the quintessential presidents in the United States of America's history, Abraham Lincoln.

During the American Civil War, Abraham Lincoln effectively led the Union against the Confederate charge, securing the freedom of millions of slaves. Looking at his life, you cannot help but wonder if the man had the nerve of steel. He failed at so many things yet became the 16th president of the United States of America.[iv]

Unlike many other presidents, Abraham Lincoln wasn't born into a wealthy family, nor did he enjoy an unproblematic ascension to the highest office of the US. With all of Lincoln's problems and failures, I was obliged to dig deeper to uncover the causes that drove his perseverance in the face of challenges and failures.

Let's recount the failures experienced by Abraham Lincoln; he was defeated for senate legislature in 1832, lost his business in 1833, was elected to the state legislature in 1834, his sweetheart died in 1835, he suffered a nervous breakdown in 1836, was defeated for house speaker in 1838, lost the nomination for Congress in 1843, elected for Congress in 1846, lost re-nomination in 1848, defeated for US Senate 1854 and defeated for nomination for Vice President of the USA in 1858. However, it was in 1860 when his resilience and efforts bore fruit, and he was elected for the office of the President.

Each time I look at the life and contribution of

Abraham Lincoln, I am reminded that failure should not be the gavel in my story. Rather it should serve as a motivation to continue working for my goals and dreams.

Abraham Lincoln suffered many career setbacks that would have sent most into hiding, but for some odd reason, he seemed to use his failure as recycled energy to fuel his commitment to purpose. His story continues to inspire millions of people worldwide who are on their own path to leadership.

After experiencing what many viewed as fatal blows to his career, it begs the question: why would Lincoln ignore the glaring reality that he's not a natural winner? Some would probably discourage his efforts by encouraging him to focus on celebrating the wins he accomplished so far and just gave up already.

Having suffered a fresh loss for a senate seat to Stephen A. Douglas in 1858, Lincoln did not let it stop him from participating in the race to the Presidential Office of the United States of America in 1860. Although he failed in the senate race to Douglas, Lincoln gained much popularity from this race itself and sought to leverage it to aim for a higher target.

Abraham Lincoln suspended his practice as a lawyer and directed his entire focus towards becoming the next President of the United States of America. I could imagine what the people around him must be saying; "If you cannot win a senate seat, why on earth would you think you can become the next president of the most powerful country on Earth?"

Yet, in another instance of defying the odds, on the 6th of November in 1860, Lincoln captured the hearts of his fellow American citizens to become the 16th President of the United States of America, winning with 180 Electoral College votes along with the popular vote.

Abraham Lincoln inherited the office to run a deeply divided country on the brink of a civil war. He led the country through one of its bloodiest wars, a period that was a defining moment in the history of America, which eventually led to the freedom of slaves.

Would there be an Emancipation Proclamation had Abraham Lincoln chosen the route that many others decided to take when staring down the barrels of failure and disappointment? The answer lies in the incident of January 1, 1863, when Abraham Lincoln came forward with a declaration that would change America forever; "All persons held as slaves are, and henceforth shall be free."

When failure is feared and perceived as the decider of our fate, opportunities for greatness are missed, and we begin pitching our tents in the land of 'what-ifs,' never to experience the greatness that can emanate from resiliently taking action.

Everyone experiences the fear of failure and the constant temptation to quit. Quitting always appears to be the easiest way out. Our unwillingness to own our role as a learner in the leadership journey and to move on with renewed strength to face new challenges with greater resolve will deprive the world of the next invention, idea, concept, or life-changing moment.

Many people would view Abraham Lincoln's advancement in his career from failing a Senate election to winning the Presidency election as a fluke; after all, it was decorated with some monumental failures. Experiencing the highs and lows during his journey left him with enough scars to force an average man into retirement. Because most of us often allow the scars of our failures to prevent us from stepping forward with confidence and clarity.

I believe I am qualified to speak on this because I've allowed myself to do this on numerous occasions. I turned down multiple promotion opportunities because I was afraid to fail by falling short of the expectations of my bosses. I recall resisting investment opportunities because the last investment I tried had resulted in a loss. I've withheld my opinions in meetings where my ideas would have made a big difference; for no other reason outside of not wanting to confront an issue on which, I believed I would be outnumbered.

There is a question that I always ask of those who gave up on their purpose out of a fear of failure; What do you do with all the goals, dreams, passion, and ideas you had burning inside you? Did you become a new person overnight after burying your passion and silencing the voice of the ideas screaming inside of you? John Maxwell wrote a book titled "Sometimes You Win. Sometimes You Learn". Abraham Lincoln and Thomas Edison clearly lived this, and so should you.

Gena Showalter puts it this way; "Giving up is the only sure way to fail."[v], and I completely agree with it. Let us accept that mustering the grit and resilience to continue after failure is challenging. It is particularly true if you view yourself as a failure and are highly concerned about what others think of your experiences.

The life of Abraham Lincoln serves as a reminder that we must not allow our failures to derail us from our purpose but instead must expose us to opportunities to learn and grow.

Enlisting Support from Others

As is true for all challenges, there is a strategy to embrace and navigate failure through a leadership journey. It is inevitable that at some point, you will face challenges and failures in areas that exceed your abilities, skillset, or current resources. These circumstances make a very compelling case for waving the white flag in surrender. As someone who embraces strategic initiatives steeped in innovation and agility, I have never allowed the absence of certain tools or skills to prevent me from overcoming failure, and neither should you.

Bouncing back is not optional, it is a necessity. It means we must be willing to seek and accept the help and support from those who have faced similar obstacles along their journeys. You may not find such individuals in your immediate circle of friends or network. Nonetheless, they can offer support, training, and mentorship, which would be just as encouraging.

During my first year of college, I enrolled in a

programming class. While I may not have the empirical evidence to support my position on this (judging from the failure rate for this class), it was a widely held view that this course of study was ranked among the toughest in the IT program.

Because of this, my friends who knew me as a natural talker and an extrovert, began encouraging me to switch majors to Media or Psychology.

However, that is when my competitive side kicked in, and I became determined to prove that I could study the subject and succeed at it. I decided to take the course. I was confident and ready to face any challenges that could arise during my journey of taking this course. However, not before long, I would be faced with the reality that this was no walk in the park.

When I received the results of my first major quiz, my lack of giftedness in programing was evident. There was so much I didn't know, and I understood and accepted the fact that I would not succeed in this class without enlisting the support and guidance of others who grasped the concepts much better than me. I also recognized that I needed to spend more time practicing outside of my class on this course if I wanted to pass.

After recognition of the need for support and guidance, my next step was to connect with a few of my classmates. This one action on my part was what changed the trajectory of my college journey. While others sought to withdraw from the class in the face of failure, I chose to take another route, and this created an experience for me that helped with all the other successes I experienced during my four-year college journey.

Bounce Back Theory

As I reflect on my own journey as a leader, I realize that I have experienced more defeats than I could have imagined. However, the failures and challenges provided proof that small wins are powerful forces to drown out the experience of failure. Sometimes, we must be intentional about identifying and celebrating these small wins.

There is a systematic way to overcome defeat. The Bounce Back Theory is a beneficial strategy that will allow you to resiliently confront failure, resiliently bounce back, and follow through on your goal. I've used this system and found it to be very helpful during times when resilience was not an option but a necessity.

There is a famous quote that goes like this; "Quitters never win, and winners never quit." I coined my own saying to match this one: "Quitters bounce, but winners bounce back and follow through." Both statements ring true when it comes to failure. It is up to us to quit or choose a path that would lead towards winning.

When children learn to walk, there come several occasions where they would fall or trip or just topple over due to their lack of balance. Could you imagine what would happen if we prevented our children from attempting after their first tumble? What if we decide to restrict them from ever trying again in our bid to protect them from getting hurt? The results would be terrible; their growth would become stunted.

Even the babies understand the necessity to bounce back and follow through after a setback, so what is stopping you? Failing at something is not a cue to stop trying. Next time you experience a failure, I would like you to practice these five steps from the Bounce Back Theory:

1. Accept your failure
2. Assess your failure
3. Anchor your attention on your purpose
4. Acquire a network of support
5. Create an 'Action Plan'

Accept your Failure

Surmounting challenges requires intentionality and effort. But before we can do this, acceptance is a very crucial step in the process of bouncing back. So if we fail to accept the failure, we might delay the progress we could possibly make from being able to put in place a response or a plan to overcome our challenges. Sometimes, the reason behind this denial is rooted in the belief that 'admitting that I failed at something, means I am a failure.' The sooner we realize that we are so much more than our failures, the faster we will come to the reality that a change is required.

This is an acknowledgment that you have made some bad decisions, sought advice from the wrong people, or lacked the required skills to conquer or confront the challenges. It is the first step to bounce back from failure and position yourself to follow through.

Some leaders believe that acceptance of failure is a

sign of weakness, but they could not be more wrong. Acceptance is the first step towards change.

Assess your Failure

After accepting the need for a change, your next step should be to take the time out to evaluate the reasons and overall impact of the failure on your journey. Failure assessment is an essential step in analyzing what not to do on the next occasion when you are confronted with a similar challenge. Monday morning quarterbacking is another term that has been used to describe this process.

Amy Edmonson suggests that on every occasion that failure is experienced, two things should be highlighted: something that is praiseworthy and something blameworthy. Essentially, her thought pattern for this kind of assessment is rooted in the belief that the failure we experience directly results from actions that should not be repeated; this action is blameworthy, and we should learn from it.

Conversely, some actions may result in failure. However, these actions are "thoughtful experimentation that generated valuable information." They are praiseworthy and must be celebrated and leveraged to support future decision-making.

Edmonson proposes that treating failure as a tabooed subject can result in losing valuable insights. It inevitably leads to a loss of opportunities to refine a process or product.

One of the most effective strategies used by NBA

coaches is a requirement for players to watch the replay of their games. It is usually done with games they've lost.

Players are required to spend hours breaking down the plays and analyzing moves that did not go according to the game plan. It is said that Kobe Bryant—one of the greatest NBA players of his generation—spent hours watching reruns of games just to be better prepared for his next encounter.

Assessing your failures signals a willingness on your part to revisit the scene of loss boldly and courageously, the place where you tasted defeat. Let's be honest, it is a traumatic experience to revisit one's failures. After all, this was the place that knocked the air out of you and left you weak and deflated before the world and yourself.

One of the hallmarks of a great leader lies in their ability to evaluate their bouts with failure, knowing fully well that if they should use the lessons learned, it will only serve to strengthen their odds of overcoming defeat when faced with similar or even greater challenges in the future.

The most essential yet daunting aspect of assessing failure is to cogitate on your own level of preparedness in an open and honest way in relation to the challenges faced. Quite often, leaders allow their pride and ego to serve as blockers to the progress they can make from open and honest reflection. They fail to leverage some of the most powerful strengths to be gleaned from vulnerability. They also fail to own what they did wrong and thus cripple their ability to improve, adjust, or reimagine their approach.

Self-evaluation is a very critical step in response to failure. Assessing your failures gives you a renewed sense of confidence to move forward and is infinitely more effective in strengthening your ability to move forward. One of the worst things that could happen is to have lost a game or failed at an assignment and choose to stay in a state of ignorance about the root cause for your failure.

Few things will adversely impact your growth, such as willful ignorance in this regard. To rise above the challenges, it is important to always be open to self-reflection. By dissecting the failures faced, we can use the insights gleaned from such assessment to grow.

Remain Anchored in your Purpose

After assessing your failure and gleaning meaningful insights into what you could do differently, you should remain anchored on your purpose. Your purpose is what defines you.

Your purpose is your reason for doing what you do. I will touch on clarity later in the book; however, when it comes to failure, your purpose is your anchor. Sometimes, when we encounter failure, depending on the degree to which we experience it, we may find ourselves shaken and disoriented from it. However, once clarity of purpose is present, it will become easier to find your way back to the success pathway.

The Olympics is an event that has captivated my attention throughout the years. The past four or five Olympics were among my favorites, because of the outstanding performances by Jamaican athletes, with

Usain St. Leo Bolt emerging as the lightning sensation who captured the hearts of people around the world.

What would have happened had Usain Bolt decided to turn his back to the field after a less than appraisable performance during the 2005 World Championship? In that race, he was placed last, behind the giants of his time, such as Tyson Gay and Justin Gatlin?

Aged only 15, Bolt was already making waves in Jamaica and many places around the world because of his irreproachable performance on the track. He had broken multiple records at such a tender age, including the Junior Championship in 2002.

With all the success he had amassed, and despite his talent, exemplary performances, and dedication, he sustained a hamstring injury, which rendered him unfit for the 200m final at the 2004 Olympics in Athens. To make matters worse, he came last in the 200m finals at the 2005 World Track and Field Championships. What if he had decided to quit and allowed his talent and dreams to drown in the loud voices of critics?

Sometimes, our strategies are not aligned with our purpose, and because of that, we fail. In such cases, we can always ditch or re-imagine that plan, but not at the cost of abandoning our purpose.

Our purpose is the compass for success and the anchor we need to keep us grounded as we stare failure in the eye. Think about it, after Usain Bolt's disappointing performance at his first Olympics and World

Championship, he was on the verge of throwing away his purpose. However, the game changed when Bolt was taken under the wings of one of Jamaica's top coaches, Glen Mills.

Once he was hired as coach, Mills shared his evaluation of Bolt as 'a talented runner with poor technique'. Glen Mills worked with Bolt on his technique, and today, we are all celebrating the fact that Bolt did not give up on his purpose. Bolt retired as the fastest man alive because he was willing to assess his failure while he remained anchored in his purpose.

Acquire a Network

There is a common saying that some have written off as clichéd, but I came to see the truth in this as part of my own leadership journey: "Your network is worth more than your net worth." People need people to grow and succeed. We all need people in our network who will be ready to provide us with feedback, encourage us when we are drifting away from our purpose, and help us to get back on track when we falter. There is a song we learned at school as children, which rings true in this context:

No man is an island,
No man stands alone,
Each man's joy is a joy to me,
Each man's grief is my own.
We need one another,
So, I will defend,
Each man as my brother,
Each man is my friend.

No one person has the skills, gifts, or physical wherewithal to do everything alone. Where our limitations end, we must surround ourselves with the kind of people that will complement and support us into becoming the very best version of ourselves.

There are some who refuse to subscribe to this notion because absorbing all the credit is far more attractive; but the African proverb could not be more profound in conveying the sentiments I share in this regard: "If you want to go fast, go alone. If you want to go far, go together".

Sometimes, you have a dream or a plan, but you don't possess the right skillset to take you to your goal. In such situations, what helps is when you have people who would be able to connect you with suitable sources and take you to the right places to attain the required skillset for the development of your goal. After interviewing several leaders for this book, not a single person claimed to have attained success as a leader without the help of a trusted guide or a mentor.

If you do not have someone you can count as a mentor, it is high time that you search for one who can support you through life's most challenging situations. There is wisdom in leveraging the attainments and insights of those who have walked the road before you.

Your network should also include a coach who is demonstrably equipped to help you expand your skills and talents beyond your imagination. Your network is the vehicle that will take you places you've never been and assist you in attaining goals that are well beyond anything you could ever imagine.

Your network should be reflective of the set of values that you embrace and who you aspire to become. When you tap into your network, you should come out electrified, inspired, and motivated to bounce back from any failure you have experienced. Your network will encourage you to ditch a plan if it is not working for you, or they may even help you to re-invent the plan so you may adjust and adapt, if necessary, on the journey towards achieving your goals.

Create an Action Plan

Once you have activated the power within your network, the next step to take is to create an action plan. Action plans add meaning and provide a roadmap for you as you chart your course away from failure. An effective action plan for winning from failures covers the following steps:

1. Clearly defined goals
2. Determine steps that must be taken to achieve these goals
3. Secure the right team of people, promoters, motivators, sponsors
4. Evaluate your steps to see if they are taking you closer to your goals
5. Set a timeline for your goals

Not having a clearly defined goal is tantamount to taking shots at a basketball hoop while being blindfolded.

You want to be intentional with your approach towards life and your purpose. Setting goals provides you with something for which you can aim every step along the way.

While having goals is important, it is important to outline the steps necessary to be taken to get to your goals. By outlining your steps, you become able to identify what needs to be placed primarily on the priority list. It is like planning a hiking trip. You must take the right gear if you plan on making it to the top of the mountain.

Many times, we failed to make it to the end zone because we did not set markers. Without markers, you are at constant risk of becoming disheartened and quitting. Having a clear idea of your next step will save you from repeating mistakes that could lead to further failure.

While steps are important, you need a team to assist you in materializing the plan. That team of people that you choose must have your interest at heart. They must be willing to support and guide you when this is required. This team is the circle that will celebrate with you, cry with you, hold you accountable, and challenge you when necessary.

The next step is to decide what you will require to determine if your plan is working or if you need to adjust your ways. At this stage, you must **evaluate your steps** and your overall strategy based on your purpose and your objective. It is where you make decisions about moving on, pulling back, or pressing forward at top speed.

There are many leaders who are so obsessed with the **fear of failure** that they might deliberately miss opportunities to avoid failure. The unwillingness to venture towards solutions out of the fear of the inevitable is one of the worst moves a leader could make.

Often, leaders shut down specific opportunities or challenges because they would like to keep a clean sheet or a clean record. It is not to imply that the leaders should be reckless, but rather, to emphasize that leadership is all about producing results. The solutions we seek to achieve this are tied to how we manage our failures or the quest to improve something.

When we allow our fear of failure to influence our decision-making, we commit one of the greatest crimes that a leader could commit; we settle for mediocrity. Do not allow your fear to dictate how you view potential failure, instead, manage your fear in a manner that becomes more of a motivating factor towards acquiring the skills which are needed to surmount the challenges.

Reflection Questions

As you reflect on your journey so far, identify some of the failures you've experienced (personally and professionally) that you handled well and or some you didn't handle so well.

- Based on what you've read so far, describe some of the benefits you experienced for the failures you managed well in your life.

- How has your fear of failure impeded your overall growth(personally and professionally)?

- What strategies will you take away from this chapter to help you better manage situations that did not go as planned.

Chapter Three: Foresight

"The best decision-makers are capable of seeing the present as if it were already the past." - Charles Schwab

Having the ability to act, think or strategize in the present and win in the future is a shared goal, which we all aspire towards. An even greater skill comes with one's ability to anticipate and put in place-responsive measures for the challenges and opportunities of the future.

We read books, listen to podcasts, attend conferences, and sign up for multiple courses, all for the purpose of making effective decisions today that will bring us the very best results tomorrow. Knowing what is coming next or being positioned to predict what will happen in the future, is a gift that many wish for. We are all searching for the right recipe that will give us an edge over the masses tomorrow.

Let's face it; we don't possess a crystal ball through which we can see the future. Foresight is not a sixth sense given to special people. This is an acquired ability that we get to hone only after spending much time and effort studying the past and the forces that work together to activate certain elements and bring about the results we want to achieve (McCain[vi]).

Wayne Gretsky was one of the greatest hockey players of all time. When asked about the secret behind his success as a player, Gretsky responded, "I skate where the puck is going to be, not where it's been."

Foresight is a skill that any person can develop if they remain committed to the right behaviors and habits, which could help shape the future we want to live in. John McCain said it best; "Genuine foresight is not the mark of some special genius that is inexplicably bestowed on a few. It is the achievement of painstaking inquiry and the disciplined application of reason to the knowledge [that] we have acquired." Here McCain insinuate that we all are capable of developing foresight as a gift, and if cultivated, foresight can lead us on a path of success and transformation.

At a glance, the dictionary definition of foresight reads as 'the ability to predict what will happen or what will be needed in the future.' In its truest sense, foresight is what helps us to prepare for and execute our plans in the way we have envisioned it, anticipating certain future events(negative and positive) so we can successfully put measures in place to capitalize on the opportunities and limit the impact of negative factors that can overwhelmingly affect our overall success.

Regardless of your talent, resources, or experience, if you fail to anticipate future challenges, your relevance, impact, or success will eventually lose value. In the quest to understand the context and significance of foresight, someone asked, "Since I can't predict the future, why is this an important aspect of my leadership journey?"

While my response to this line of inquiry is simple—it is not simplistic; because without foresight, you will never be able to envision and experience the best version of yourself, you will not know when this has been achieved, and consequently, you fail to attain and maintain such a monumental achievement.

When it comes to the future, there are certain habits or principles that we must embody while keeping the future at the forefront of our minds. Peter Schwartz offers an interesting take on this subject in his book *The Art of the Longview.* What he essentially says is, the need to be present now also means that you can perceive what the future holds and evaluating how present circumstances are preparing you to be successful when you get there.[vii]

Your ability to standout or dominate in your respective areas of specialty requires intentionality. There must be a willingness to create just enough space between you and the present, and invest the time, effort, and energy into carving out the future that you want to live in.

You must have the capacity to view everything with an unbiased, curious, reflective, and innovative eye. Undoubtedly, success in this area is inextricably linked to your ability to master these key skills and strategies so that you can enjoy a front-row seat to the future: a guaranteed path to relevance, success, and sustained impact.

In this manner, you will be able to engage in one of the most consequential strategies within the realm of foresight: gap leadership and scenario planning. We will take a deeper dive into scenario planning further ahead in this chapter.

Gap Leadership

The concept of *Gap Leadership* came to me during an early morning walk as I came across a gaggle of geese making their way across the soccer field. I took keen note of the leader, who consistently maintained a distance ahead of the gaggle.

They followed him at every turn. As leaders, we must always have a space where we are a few steps ahead of our team. Gap leadership gives you the freedom to assess the path ahead, so you can effectively lead your team to success. The more time we spend in the weeds, the more we rob our team of an opportunity to benefit from visionary and strategic leadership.

What does Gap Leadership look like? It's taking time out to remain on the cutting edge by engaging with a variety of reading materials on topics that are relevant to your industry and leadership. It requires time away from the office and out of the trenches to attend conferences and retreats that will revitalize and infuse your leadership with new life.

What Happens in the Absence of Foresight?

One of my college friends once told me that he did not see much value in thinking a lot about the future. I asked him to share his reasons for this, to which his reply was: "Thinking about the future is a waste of valuable time that could be better spent appreciating the present."

While I can appreciate his supporting argument, I observed some dangers relative to this perspective. If we limit ourselves to only thinking about and planning for our present opportunities, we will essentially miss out on future opportunities that could only be attained by intentional effort.

Many times, we fail to exercise foresight because we are unwilling to embrace any thought that requires us to adjust or adapt to any form of change. That fear of exercising foresight will inevitably lead to:

1. Loss of relevance
2. Extinction
3. Lack of personal and professional growth and development
4. Missed opportunities
5. Lack of preparation for the inevitable

Loss of Relevance

When relevance is lost, you will be relegated into antiquity. Even if you have amassed great successes, you will only be able to remain relevant if there is a demand for what you have to offer. To avoid the loss of relevance, a leader must consistently leverage the key tenets of foresight to keep them prepared for future needs and challenges. By doing this, they will remain in a position where their gifts and talents are constantly being sought-after.

Growing up in a small community, I witnessed first-hand, on multiple occasions, the failures faced by small businesses and corner stores due to their inability to remain relevant. These businesses opened their doors to meet a specific community's needs, but they failed to remain on the cutting edge of emerging trends, particularly amongst their target groups.

Once there was an active need for their services, they did well, but when the dust settled, they struggled to keep the business alive. The reason was their unwillingness to change with the times. Looking back, I realize that it was not a bad location or the lack of patrons that led to most start-up businesses shutting down. Instead, it was the fact that they failed to exercise the foresight necessary to remain relevant, and their customers outgrew them as a result.

I often share with friends, clients, and business leaders that they should never allow the lack of foresight to be the determining factor for the end of their businesses, ambitions, or goals. If we succeed in unlocking the power that is inherent within this amazing principle, the possibilities will be endless.

Whether you find yourself in an entry-level, managerial, specialist, or individual contributor role, there is always something of value that we all bring to these jobs. We are actively fulfilling a need. Once that need is diminished or becomes non-existent, so will the services we provide. Whenever this happens, the process of extinction begins.

Foresight offers you the window into the future. Once we remain imaginative, we can anticipate what comes next and take the steps necessary to meet the changing needs on the horizon. Without that vantage point, we will be at a disadvantage. If you don't believe me, you might want to investigate companies like Kodak, Nokia, and Blockbuster and see what they all have in common.

Avoiding the Risk of Extinction

Lack of relevance is just one of the results of lack of foresight. In addition to the loss of relevance, one should also be mindful of the possibility of extinction. Yes, I did use the word extinction. I am aware that this is a word often associated with endangered species or even animals like the saber-tooth cats and Tasmanian tigers.

It is safe to assume that most of us share the dream of building a legacy that will transcend our own lifetime and one that we can truly be proud of. When we die, we hope to leave behind a legacy that will live on in our children. Extinction poses a direct threat to that legacy. One of the best ways to become extinct is to become so immersed in what is currently going on that we have little time and energy to invest in future-building behaviors.

We don't ever intentionally immerse ourselves in the business of the moment while paying little or no attention to what comes next. However, so many of us find ourselves trapped in the endless cycle of being engrossed in the here and now, giving ourselves little time to strategize, plan and dream for the future.

Facing an ever-changing future forces leaders to prepare not only to meet the challenges but also to be positioned in such a way that they will capitalize on opportunities that will come their way.

The interesting thing about life is that the emergence of new challenges is inextricably linked to new needs. Those of us who will survive, nay thrive, are those who are willing to rise to the occasion and meet the moment with a strategy that will position us as the best person or entity to fulfill that need.

An unwillingness to develop foresight and use it as a guiding principle will inevitably place you in the extinction lane. Such individuals forego successes that were once within their reach or hold fast to past successes that are incapable of sustaining them in a place of prominence and relevance.

The very best definition I've heard of success was given by one of my all-time favorite speakers – Zig Ziglar. He defines success as 'the intersection between preparation and opportunity.[viii]' Opportunity follows need just as sure as dusk follows dawn.

In our consulting practice, we champion the art of stretching. Whether physically, mentally, or socially, stretching is an essential part of our existence as human beings. Within the context of foresight, a commitment to grow personally will help us resist the boredom of complacency and mediocrity.

As is the case with the loss of relevance, and the risk of extinction, it doesn't take a great deal of effort to miss out on personal development opportunities; maintaining the status quo most certainly will do that for us. Growth will only come as we intentionally take the steps necessary to move beyond what we know now and who we are by remaining curious and seeking to evolve into new and improved versions of ourselves. Foresight forces us to remain curious, as a result, making us into a significant and dominant force, not within just an organization but also before the world at large.

Missed Opportunities

Lack of foresight can lead to missed opportunities, especially during a crisis. My friend Noel reached out to me at the beginning of the COVID-19 pandemic. He suggested that I should start doing research into companies that are developing vaccines for the novel Coronavirus. He even went the extra mile by suggesting a particular stock that he thinks may have some potential.

I must be honest, this early into the pandemic, I wasn't intrigued by the idea at the time. It did not feel like a financial priority. Additionally, I couldn't make a significant financial investment. Thus, I tabled the idea. Within a month of that phone call, I received another call from Noel. Previously, he had suggested that I should purchase the stock, the rate per share was $20.

When he called me a month later, the cost per share for the stock was now $54.00. It was most certainly a very costly opportunity that I failed to capitalize on. I eventually got into the market, but I was late. Like me, you too will miss opportunities of a lifetime if you fail to allow foresight to play a significant role in the way you act and make decisions.

Have you ever attempted an exam, attended a meeting, or gave a speech, while being completely unprepared? I have experienced the pinch of unpreparedness and its painful. It is one of the worst feelings I've ever experience. The tune of 'shoulda-coulda-woulda' replays over and over in my mind like a broken record. I thought about all the things I could have done that would have resulted in a much better outcome.

The same can be said about life, leadership, and whatever area of service you find yourself in. There are some changes that are predictable, while others will throw us a curveball. Being able to predict the change or be in the most solid position to withstand a curveball is the definition of preparation.

When we listen to the weather forecast and receive forewarning of a rainy day, it's always a good feeling to take along with you an umbrella as you venture out into the world. Even if the prediction was wrong, you are in a much better position to face the rain than you would have been without an umbrella, if the prediction turned out to be accurate.

The most important thing to remember is that the accuracy of the forecast is secondary to having a forecast. Forecasts provides an opportunity to plan and prepare for the day ahead. Just like the weather, change is one of constants that we must contend with, and those of us who will be on the cutting edge when it comes, are the ones who will be positioned for greatness.

Foresight in Action

When I think about foresight, the first person that comes to mind is the founder and CEO of the world's largest e-commerce business, Jeff Bezos. Not only is he one of the world's wealthiest people, but Jeff Bezos has also shaped the way we buy and sell goods for ages to come. Within this lifetime, Amazon stands as a giant amidst a field of successfully run organizations.

In 1994, Bezos and his friends started an online bookstore from his garage, and in eight years, he had expanded his business offerings to include to selling music, clothing, and web hosting services. From one unpopular move to another, Jeff Bezos allowed his foresight to fuel his innovation. With his out-of-the-box thinking, he achieved the consistent success and transformation we see today. When the world thought that Jeff Bezos was comfortable with the numerous achievements he had amassed, he came forth with a surprise; by adding the delivery line to his operations[ix].

While we celebrate his success today, Bezos is known as a visionary. He made some unpopular decisions, but he was willing to live with the results of what the unchartered territory had to offer. His achievements are now being hailed out-of-this-world.

On Becoming a Leader of Foresight

Many people would have you think that you must be born with this special gift, which couldn't be further from the truth. Regardless of your background, you can become a leader of foresight. It is a skill that can be developed, and like any skill, the more you practice, the better you become at it.

Becoming a leader of foresight really comes down to three important factors: confronting your biases, building self-awareness, and leveraging the power of curiosity.

Confronting Your Biases

World-renowned astronomer and cosmologist Carl Sagan cautions us to "try not to get overly attached to a hypothesis, just because it's ours.[x]" This statement, to me, is the very essence of open-mindedness and having an unbiased approach to life. Many of us are imprisoned by our biases, which impairs our ability to see the broader picture of the world and prevents us from viewing the world as it is and not what it could become. This does not imply that you are not entitled to an opinion, or you shouldn't place value on your unique way of thinking.

I often share with the clients I coach the value of using their eyes, ears, and arms to embrace the growth mindset. It is important to open your eyes to see what others are doing, to open your arms to welcome things that are different, or, in some cases, unfamiliar, but in the long run, will give you the tools you need to be successful, and open your ears to hear what others are thinking. In other words, our senses are crucial in the discernment of new and emerging ideas that are different from what we are accustomed to.

Letting go of our biases is not a simple walk in the park. It takes painstaking effort to let go of the things you deem right and safe. The important question to consider, though, as you rehearse the difficulty of letting go, is: "What if letting go is just the step I need to take to make it to the destination I seek?"

The first and probably the most challenging step we can take to achieve this is always to remain open to the evaluation of our personal beliefs. The important thing about   evaluating   our is that while engaged in this process, we must ask ourselves questions like, "Why do I even believe in this in the first place?"

Fast-food is not my favorite, and I could live on home-cooked meals for the rest of my life. However, on the occasions that I dine out, I try to make life very easy for those who serve me. I am very clear on my preferences, and my order is usually the same on most occasions.

The sad part about this approach is that I've missed numerous opportunities to experience and taste the other delectable options on the menu. Like me, some of us make it through life and business with this approach and have missed out on the opportunity to have our lives enriched because we remain shackled to our preferences.

On one occasion, as I completed my order, my wife turned to me and said, "Jaymie, you are so predictable." It felt like a gut punch, even though I had to admit to myself that she was right. Her comment forced me to pause and reflect. The next time I went to order, I could hear my wife's voice reverberating in my ear, and this pushed me to explore the other sections of the menu.

The trait of being predictable was not one I was happy to be associated with. Especially when this association is being made by my wife. As a result of self-reflection, I have made it a habit to switch between food items after that day. I try to experiment a little, even if it means I am changing up just the sauce.

Because of my adventurous exploits around menus, I was able to unlock the heavenly taste of the pineapple cheesecake empanadas from Bahama Breeze and the delectable avocado rolls from the Cheesecake Factory.

We stand to lose so much when we stay married to our personal preferences, and we can do this to the detriment of those we serve and those we hope to serve in the future.

Because our preferences are shaped primarily by our experiences and socialization, we must find ways to constantly question the reasons for which we have developed these preferences in the first place.

As aspiring leaders, we must be reminded that we will serve people from all walks of life, and it is critical for them to feel like we value their preferences. A willingness to explore what lies beyond our personal preferences will allow us to take risks and make better decisions as we seek to garner success through human systems.

This one question is an admission that some of the beliefs and norms we hold are like old relics that lack the power to advance us along our success journey. Any deeply held belief system that adds no value to our lives should be dismissed and replaced with values that better serve our ability to grow personally. We should stop wasting time and energy preserving what no longer serves us.

Confronting Mental Shortcuts

We should take no hesitation in confronting our mental shortcuts. I have discovered in my own journey that some of the things I considered to be a shorter route to get to what I needed was not short, but, in fact, longer and relatively more demanding and unproductive. It is the result when we become overly comfortable while doing things a particular way. Though there may be somethings that are seemingly more familiar or are within our comfort zone, it does not necessarily guarantee the outstanding results we seek.

The fact is that most of the time, the success we seek resides outside our comfort zone. Choosing to hire someone who went to the same college as you did, just because you are acquainted with the quality of their education or choosing someone to be on a cross-functional team project merely based on familiarity, may not necessarily be the key to creating that dream team you are in search of.

Familiarity feels good, but by the same token, it can serve as a shackle – limiting your ability to grow and expand your horizon. Sometimes, you must choose the tougher route, the road less traveled, and confront your mental shortcuts. When there is a willingness to do this, it will also help you evaluate the factors that drive your preferences.

Embrace Meaningful Differences

Embracing anything outside of our comfort zone can be painstakingly difficult because it goes against our innate fight-or-flight defense mechanisms. This system is in place to protect us from things that we consider to be different, and sometimes it can serve as a double-edged sword, causing us to act in an ambivalent or indifferent manner towards any sight of change on the horizon.

Some of us were explicitly and implicitly taught through our experiences to resent differences. As we talked about failure in the previous chapter and the impact of the bounce back theory, we recognize that the only way to move forward successfully at times may call for us to evaluate the differences in an approach that can have a meaningful and positive impact on our lives.

My wife's uncle shared an experience that has profoundly impacted his perception of life and success. He was a silent observer at a board meeting for a popular food chain in Jamaica. The CEO was seated at the head of his boardroom table, observing the ongoing discussion about a waste management challenge that his multi-million-dollar food chain faced. He was becoming more and more resentful of the fact that the item had been on the agenda for two months without a resolution.

They were hemorrhaging cash in their attempts to outsource the job to contractors or relying on the governmental organization (who rarely showed up) to collect the waste. It resulted in piles of trash at the location, which started to give off a stench and became a bother at that site.

The leadership was flooded with numerous complaints from neighboring businesses and customers alike. They needed to come up with a solution to keep their stakeholders happy, and they had very little time to attain that objective.

Within 25 minutes of the discussion, the janitor walked into the board room to empty the wastebasket. An idea popped into the mind of the CEO, who then silenced the room. His voice was elevated above everyone else in the room as he turned his attention to the janitor.

"Mr. Jackson, what do you think we can do to address the waste management issue at the dumpster?" The janitor responded, "With all the money we have been spending, I would just buy a truck instead and hire a driver." In all the discussions so far, no one thought about that as an option. However, the CEO was willing to take a risk on someone who was not in a senior role on the board. The janitor's recommendation was what helped the company to resolve the long-standing issue.

Sometimes we measure diversity within the realm of race, culture, gender, etc., but diversity also has to do with differences in roles and experiences that can help us see things from a completely different perspective.

Though the upfront cost to purchase a garbage truck seemed like the most unlikely alternative, it was a worthwhile investment in the long run. Much of what was lost was not just related to dollars and cents but other qualitative factors, such as the reputation of the organization and the interest of the stakeholders.

As we begin to embrace the meaningful differences, our perception expands beyond our own worldview. It also empowers us to take on a not-so-familiar path that will provide us with a new and different perspective.

In his book, *The 15 Invaluable Laws of Growth*, John Maxwell says, "You have to glance backward and plan forward." I found this quote to be meaningful when exercising the power of foresight. An awareness of where you are coming from while focusing on where you are heading is a crucial aspect of securing results. In chapter three of this book, we will further elaborate on the concept of awareness and its importance in a leadership journey and success.

The Role of Ambition in Developing Foresight

Mark Twain has a word of advice for ambitious leaders: "Keep away from those who try to belittle your ambitions. Small people always do that, but only the great make you believe that you too can become great." [xi] Millions of ideas and dreams die on the vine every day because ambitions are never encouraged.

Ambition has a transformative effect when it comes on to foresight. It's kind of a "get-up-and-go" element to a thought or idea. It provides you with the energy to stubbornly pursue a dream or goal and enables you to avoid procrastination and complacency.

Sometimes, others may not be able to see what you see because of their own limitations, but they can sense your passion and commitment to bring these things to life. Kobe Bryant, Michael Jordon, and Mohammad Ali were all ambitious leaders. Just like them, you have the potential to leverage the power of ambition and win on a consistent basis.

The drive to achieve or experience something will sometimes force you to think of ways to bring the ideas to life consistently. I count ambition as that driving force in overcoming obstacles that may arise in pursuit of one's goals. The dictionary definition for ambition is "the strong desire to achieve something, typically requiring determination and hard work." xii When we unite the force of ambition with foresight, the major hindrances from our pathway to success are automatically eliminated.

Those, who are driven by this powerful force, will make a way even in the face of detractors. They will see plans and ideas for the impact and influence they will have, not for what it currently looks like.

I often ask this basic question from people; Are you determined to achieve your goals? For some, that is a difficult question because they have never taken the time to honestly evaluate their ambitions and the role that they should play in the execution of their goals. When you can plan it, feel it, and envision it, there is nothing that can stop you from achieving it.

Before Michael Jordan, LeBron James, and Steph Curry bucketed those buzzer-beating shots, they envisioned themselves doing it.

They had the ambition of winning and dominating their respective fields even before the world knew their names. That ambition was the driving force behind the passion we now see, and they were led to do what was necessary to achieve it. Like them, we should spend time evaluating our own ambitions. But I dare you to go a step further by doing something daily that brings you closer to the destination you seek.

Strategy for Foresight:
Unlocking the Power of Scenario Planning

According to Peter Schwartz, Scenario planning is about "making choices today with an understanding of how they may turn out". This is precisely the tool that allow leaders of foresight to appear as though they have read the playbook on failure. Scenario planning allows leaders to anticipate the opportunities and threats related to a plan or idea, assessing all possible outcomes[xiii].

When you master the art of scenario planning, you can set up contingencies that will successfully reduce the impact of a threat or capitalize on a potential opportunity. When done right, scenario planning will make you a winner time and again. Here, the idea is to hope for the best but plan for the worst. We should never allow future uncertainty to scare us into inaction.

In the absence of a strategy like a scenario planning, we could set ourselves up for wasted resources, disappointment, and missed opportunities. In the book *"The Art of the Long View,"* Peter Schwartz suggested a six-step approach for unlocking the best results as part of the scenario planning process, I've summarized them into four steps here:

1. Identify the objective you wish to achieve

2. Identify the future events or factors that can affect your plan, goal or decision.

3. Organize the impact of these factors base on three future possibilities:

   a. If things go as planned

   b. Things turned out differently from the way you planned but better

   c. Things end up worse than you planned

4. Derive a strategy for each of the possibilities mentioned in step three and be prepared to act on them in each scenario.

Seven Steps to Cultivating Foresight

There was a time in my life when I felt the need to work on my foresight muscle. I was making good decisions, but I failed to secure the level of impact and success that I required. In my observation and communications with successful leaders, I was informed that few of the prerequisites to becoming effective at leadership were linked to experience and age.

I found it challenging to settle for that response. Deep down, I was aware that neither of these two factors on their own could possibly guarantee the level of productivity evident in their performance. In fact, I have worked with several other colleagues who are advanced in both age and experience, but they lacked foresight.

For us to be able to successfully incorporate foresight as part of our leadership practice, Larocci suggested a few steps that I thought are also worth mentioning as part of this discussion[xiv]:

1.   **Deliberately embrace the variety.** Earlier, we spoke about the dangers of being enslaved by our preferences. When it comes to foresight, we must also know that convenience and preferences can stand in the way of our progress. Therefore, it is crucial to engage and embrace people from different backgrounds. Diversity will expand your horizon in cultural awareness and enable you to have a wider impact and influence.

Deliberately embracing variety will empower your vision to cover your blind spots, legs to go the extra mile, and wings where you need to fly—to serve, influence, and understand the struggles and preferences of others.

2. **Pay close attention to what others have to say.** Never discount what others have to say before giving them the opportunity to share. As they share, you should genuinely listen. Sometimes, the people we consider to be the least knowledgeable on a specific subject matter can provide counsel, which, if considered, can have a transformational impact on our decisions.

3. **Engage a variety of content:** Do not allow yourself to stick with books or newspapers that only appeal to your preferences, beliefs, and interests. After all, the world today is more interconnected than ever before, and reading will take you places you could not experience physically.

Confirmation bias is real. If we limit ourselves to the content that supports our worldviews, we will not benefit from the wealth of perspectives that could further enrich our leadership experience.

4. Think systemically. When you think in a systemic way, you can trace your decisions and pattern of thought in a more logical way. If this type of thinking brings you success, you can replicate and execute the same steps in the future. Within a system, an action in the present usually causes a reaction in the future. It allows you to anticipate roadblocks and potential opportunities.

5. With the support of experience and research, make guessing a habit. Numerous organizations and leaders use big data analytics as a significant element in their decision-making process. After years of measuring and analyzing key data sources, your comfort level becomes strengthened, which prepares you to make calculated guesses regarding certain decisions.

When we establish certain patterns, we can confidently form conclusions that are well-supported and more likely to be accurate, despite there being a possibility of going wrong.

6. Widen and diversify your circle of friends. Again, the old African proverb rings true; "If you want to go fast, go alone. If you want to go far, go together". Evaluate your friendship circle. Does it only comprise of people that look, think, and act like you? Then, you are running the risk of impairing your ability to make meaningful connections and decisions, which could lead to your success.

7. Reflect on the past while strategizing for the future. Embracing your past successes is not a bad thing. The challenge comes when you become so immersed in the celebration that you allow life to pass you by. We must seek to build and develop an affinity for what comes next. Our past experiences can be educational and informative, but they are not the sole authority on how we proceed into the future.

Foresight allows you to climb your way to relevance, success, and transformation. It also empowers you to see things before they happen and provide solutions for the problems of tomorrow while positioning yourself for success. Anybody can get in the game, but only those who exercise foresight are able to experience sustainable growth.

Reflection Questions – Foresight

- Describe an experience on your leadership journey in which your lack of foresight has prevented you from securing the best results?

- How could some of the strategies we discussed such as scenario planning or gap leadership help you to achieve the goals you set out to achieve?

- What steps will you take moving forward to become a leader of foresight?

Chapter Four: Awareness

"If you don't know yourself...you can't grow yourself"
– John Maxwell

Awareness is one of the most important currencies both a seasoned and an emerging leader can have as they navigate the rugged terrains of leading themselves and others. A significant amount of the failures we experience in our businesses, relationships, and projects directly result from our lack of self-awareness.

Some of my greatest disappointments or failures were not because of my lack of talent but because I was unaware. Conversely, I have had significant successes in some areas of my life, not because I was good at it, but because I was aware.

Leading Yourself

In his podcast: *The Self-Aware Leader*, John Maxwell made one of the most powerful statements I have heard on this subject[xv]. He shared, "The most difficult part of my leadership is leading myself." As leaders, we are not merely responsible for leading those who work beside, below, and above us, but also ourselves.

Awareness provides us with an aerial view of our

strengths and potential blind spots to prepare us to work diligently in the future to avoid getting in our own way when it comes to our success. Lawrence Bossidy said it best; "Self-awareness gives you the capacity to learn from your mistakes as well as your successes. It enables you to keep growing"[xvi], and I could not agree more.

Awareness is the best place to start on one's leadership journey. Before I even engage a coaching client as part of the coaching process, I always administer a scientific-based Behavioral Assessment. The objective results and insights gleaned from such an assessment is very useful and instructive in the coaching process.

If I put before you a question like: "What are some of the things that you do well?" What would be your response? Would it be something that would roll off the tip of your tongue with ease? When you are aware of the specific strengths you bring to a team, you can confidently settle into a role and perform in a way that the needs of your team are successfully met.

Ask About the Back of my T-Shirt

Mike Zani is the CEO of the Predictive Index. I attended their annual talent optimization conference, Optima, back in 2021. Mike showed up to the interview wearing a t-shirt that read, "Ask about the back of my t-shirt." That immediately caught my attention, and apparently, Guy Raz also found it to be quite intriguing as the interviewer.

"Hey, Mike, what's up with the back of your t-shirt?" Guy asked. Mike explained a concept that blew my mind. It is a concept that is fundamentally based on our personal awareness. It captures the overall perception that people have of us.

The front of our t-shirt represents the great things people readily see in us. We get promoted, applauded, or respected because of what's on the front of our t-shirts. We receive complimentary remarks because of the characteristics which the front of our apparel displays. However, we all have things on the back of our t-shirt that can have the opposite effect on our followership, message, and ability to influence and inspire others. The million-dollar question is: "Do we know what is on the back of our t-shirts?"

Are we aware of the things those other members on our team find extremely annoying about us but have never shared for fear of hurting our feelings or coming off as disrespectful? Are you conscious of the things in your behavior that are a complete turn-off for others and will cause you to come off as intimidating instead of motivating or inviting?

The truth is, whatever is on the back of our t-shirt may very well be preventing us from spring-boarding our team over that high-performance hurdle. It might even be the element preventing us from landing that promotion. It is that one thing that our superiors are saying about us when we are not in the room, and we are obliged to figure out what that "thing" is.

Regardless of the time, effort, or energy we invest in personal growth, we are bankrupt without self-awareness.

Some people are seeking to contribute at higher levels within their organization by practicing flattery or people-pleasing. It is a recipe for disaster. Some of the recent research data supports the case for awareness. According to [xvii] Golman and Boyatz, a hundred percent of leaders with a heightened sense of awareness experienced significant growth in terms of workplace effectiveness.

Light Amid Darkness

I invite you to engage in this exercise with me. Imagine that you have been invited to an old medieval castle somewhere in Europe. The goal of the trip is for you to assist with locating a lost treasure, which is believed to have been missing for centuries. There is no speculation; it is a well-known fact that the treasure is inside the castle. You find out that this treasure is believed to be worth hundreds of millions of dollars.

After receiving all the items needed for the search, the person who has extended the challenge informs you of a significant twist. The castle's architectural design causes it to be pitch-dark, and you will have to navigate its hallways to find this missing treasure without light. In that scenario, what would be the value of a single candle, lantern, or any kind of light source to you?

It goes without saying that any kind of light would prove valuable. Well, much like that light, awareness will illuminate your path on your success journey. Regardless of how small this light is, it can be helpful with vision, clarity, and the ability to surmount obstacles in your way as you go after that treasure.

When faced with setbacks, conflict, and challenges, it can be deflating, especially when we are not aware of the root cause of those challenges and how our unique strengths can help us surmount these challenges.

Awareness can serve as that light in the darkroom and become your best tool to determine where you are regarding where you need to be. When armed with this information, it will undoubtedly put you in a better position to lead yourself, as well as others.

The Power of Tendencies

Humans are very complex. We are the sum of our experiences, genetics, cultures, and environments. To ignore the role of these elements in our lives would be a mistake and one that we must avoid at all costs during our leadership journey. While they are not excuses to justify or explain destructive behaviors, our tendencies have a significant impact on our behavior and perspectives.

Our natural inclination towards a certain behavior is one definition for our "tendencies." The manifestations of these tendencies usually fall into one of the following categories:

1. Cultivated.
2. Inherited.

When you think about your cultivated tendencies, you should ask yourself, what are some of the things you've learned that have impacted the way you think, act, and make decisions. Cultivated tendencies tend to take shape as a natural response to our culture and environment.

When we engage in certain behaviors, the responses we receive tell us whether it is a positive behavior worth repeating or the opposite. Awareness is what helps us to effectively evaluate these responses so that we can make the necessary adjustments. This awareness also helps as we unlearn certain things that do not serve us well along our success journey.

What are some of the tendencies that you have nurtured which are yielding great results? What are some tendencies you have been nurturing for a long time but have placed you at odds with your team, relationships, and goals?

There are times when the blame for our lack of growth and productivity lies squarely with the things we are harboring and idolizing. James Allen, in his book "As a Man Thinketh," quotes, "We are all farmers, and whatever we sow in our garden of life will bring forth fruits. Be careful of the seeds you sow and guard your vineyard with your life[xviii]". The practical application of this quote plays a crucial role in the development of self-awareness, as we set our sights on the achievement of personal and professional goals

Inherited Tendencies

Each of us inherited behaviors, beliefs, biases, genes, and mindsets that cause us to approach things based on our parents or the first leaders we have been exposed to. Sometimes, the things we inherit through nature or nurture have a very profound impact on the way we approach life. These are the factors that drive our inherited tendencies, whether for the good or bad. These tendencies have positive and negative implications for our overall goals and objectives.

Letting go of a belief system or a way of thinking passed on to you by your parents can be challenging. It is something that you have grown to hold as the absolute truth. Let's be frank, not all inheritances are good. We should make a deliberate and conscious effort to ensure that we grow away from the tendencies that serve to negatively impact our leadership and influence.

Possessing a predisposition based on genetics to behave a certain way can threaten your success if you are unaware of its impact. Sometimes, we hear people say things like, "my father was just like that. I can't help myself". Being aware of the tendencies you have inherited, and filtering them through sociological ideals, is the first step in the right direction. It is never acceptable to excuse bad behaviors with the notion that "this is just the way I am" or "I am my father's child."

Some experts and psychologists have supported the fact that children inherit the dispositions and tendencies of their parents and imitate their behaviors. [xix] Most of the behavioral traits that we exhibit today are inherited behaviors, which we chose to imitate during the primary developmental phase of our lives. Our eyes and ears are the channels that feed our minds and instruct our thoughts and the way we view the world and those in it.

Some of my greatest failures came because I was

stuck on my inherited and cultivated tendencies. I found it difficult to live outside of that space, and in my mind, I thought I was doing well. It was not until I made a deliberate decision to make myself aware of the impact of these tendencies on my overall growth and development that I truly realized how wrong I had been. It took the wisdom of my wife to make me aware of this. There comes a time when you must assess things for their impact

Awareness is like turning on a fluorescent light in a room after you have been using a candle. It can be that tool in your arsenal that shatters glass ceilings and breaks barriers. As I reflect on my life, most of the opportunities I have missed, or the bad advice I've listened to, were not because good advice was unavailable; but because I fixed my undivided focus on what was familiar.

There comes a time when you must remove that blindfold and embrace the real you. When you learn about your strengths and potential blind spots, you can thoughtfully and strategically leverage your strengths while minimizing the impact of the blind spots on your journey.

The comfort of safety and certainty can cause us to remain stuck in our old ways. It forces us to remain married to any tendencies that we feel have served us well in the past. We need to make the transition and begin investing in and developing new and better behaviors that will help us grow.

Brandon Burchard, in his book *High-Performance Habits*, acknowledges this. He says, "Certainty is the enemy of growth and high performance. Certainty ultimately blinds you, causing you to set false and fixed limits.[xx]"

A Leader of Awareness: Mohammed Ali

Mohammed Ali's comeback fight against the hard-hitting, undefeated world champion George Foreman is evidence of the power of Awareness. Growing up, I had a much-heightened sense of admiration for Ali. Obsessed with his dominance and greatness as a fighter and showman, I was eager to discover the secrets behind Mohammed Ali's comeback fight.

October 30, 1970, in Kinshasa, Zaire (now the Democratic Republic of the Congo), the world waited with bated breath to witness the biggest boxing clash of the twentieth century. The World Heavyweight defending Champion, George Foreman, was about to defend his title against the former world champion Mohammed Ali. This fight was dubbed the *Rumble in the Jungle*, as more than 60,000 fans turned up to witness the fight[xxi].

This boxing match attracted a further 60 million viewers around the world. Mohammed Ali was recently stripped of his world championship title after refusing to fight in the Vietnam War. He had recently lost his most recent fights to two former champions and was expected to lose his bout against the young, ferocious, hard-hitting George Foreman.

During the days leading up to the fight, Mohammed Ali could be seen in the local community with the natives running and chanting, "Mohammed Ali will be killing

George Foreman in the ring." On the other hand, George Foreman remained in seclusion and chose not to socialize with the local culture or get acclimated with the weather as he prepared for his fight.

For the first four rounds of the fight, I could imagine that the world must have thought that Ali had lost his rhythm, as he was busy absorbing punches from Foreman while using the ropes of the boxing ring to escape the full measure of the blows. Not before long, there came a drastic shift in the eighth round as Mohammed Ali flipped the switch and began to dominate the young but powerful George Foreman. It was not long before the former champion knocked out the reigning champion, and the audience broke in gasps. Ali was declared the greatest boxer of all time.

Ali knew that George Foreman was a heavy-hitting boxer, and his hits were dangerous. He also knew that George Foreman had won his most recent fights by knockouts and did so in four or fewer rounds. He was also mindful of the fact that George Foreman had not been engaged in any recent fights that went beyond four rounds. He understood that all he needed to do was allow the fight to go beyond Foreman's comfort zone.

Now, that brought Foreman where he needed him. Ali leveraged his punches as well as the extreme African heat to land himself a world championship that day. To quote his own words, "He floated like a butterfly, and he stung like a bee, and the world crowned a new champion that morning."

Ali masterfully unlocked the power of awareness to secure that championship. Like him, you can secure many victories by merely developing a willingness to learn more about yourself and others to successfully navigate the rugged terrain of leadership.

Initially, the fight was Foreman's to lose. He was younger, faster, stronger, undefeated, and the favorite among most sports commentators. Mohammed Ali's understanding of George Foreman as a fighter caused him to strategically align his game plan and strategies for the fight of the century. On the day of the fight, Ali's awareness of himself, his opponent, his environment, and the steps he needed to take to win was as clear as day.

According to Scott Belsky, "Self-Leadership is about awareness, tolerance, and not letting your own natural tendencies limit your potential.[xxii]" I consider self-awareness to be the lens for leadership, the code for success, and the key that helps us unlock insights into our strengths and potential blind spots.

Self-awareness places you in an advantageous position. It empowers and enlightens those who have it in them to think and act in ways that anticipate the challenges ahead. It enables you to plan an appropriate response effectively.

Our shared beliefs and values can have a profound impact on the way we view life, make decisions and approach personal and professional challenges and opportunities. These values are shaped through our socialization and are inextricably linked to the norms and patterns to which we belong.

The values we hold dear help determine what is worthy and acceptable and what needs to be discarded. On the other hand, beliefs provide a person with a concept of what is held to be true, which is not limited to a single aspect of one's overall being.

Values, which we inherit from our culture, heavily impact our thought processes, assumptions and inclinations while making decisions and materializing them. Our cultural values will, sometimes, prevent us from doing things that would otherwise have been very easy to do due to our natural yearnings. People sometimes use their understanding of your beliefs and value system to predict what you might or might not do.

Awareness of the cultural factors that drive our behavior is critical to our overall success. Understanding your identity from a cultural standpoint provides you with an informed perspective and an opportunity to adjust, celebrate, or reinforce certain beliefs and values based on the potential impact that it could have on various groups and organizations.

Often, we limit our potential based on the cultural expectations that are placed upon us. Some of these expectations are unrealistic and might serve to cripple our ability to grow. Breaking free from such restrictions can be difficult and, at times, unacceptable by those who uphold them.

Being an outcast is not a coveted spot to be in. It is true that we live below our potential to secure the acceptance of those we love. The fact is that cultural norms shape us as individuals. We are all a living expression of our culture, whether chosen, inherited, integrated, or adopted. We are mere reflectors of the experiences and values to which we have been exposed.

Understanding your culture and the role it plays in the way you think, act, and make decisions, will go a long way in forming your need to adjust and make changes where necessary. As I reflect on some of the major decisions that I have made in my life, especially in the early stages of my leadership, I have come to the recognition that my culture has played a very significant role in impacting my worldview.

For example, as a Jamaican raised in a rich culture with national pride, I've had to resist, on numerous occasions, the temptation to brag about my home country while unwittingly minimizing other cultures.

It took some amount of empathy to allow me to recognize this as a toxic trait. Although such a practice is quite common in my culture, I had to pivot and imagine how I would feel if I were told that my cultural practices were inferior to others. Because I knew my answer to the question was a resounding no, I had to train myself not to engage in this type of behavior with people from other cultures.

Culture Impacts Expectations

Whereas the expectations within our culture affect how we behave, we can also rest assured that our culture does have an impact on what we expect of others. Sometimes, the expectations we have of people in our lives and the people we work with are based on cultural norms.

The real difficulty emerges as we come face to face with differences in other cultures. Our expectations may positively or negatively shape the way we view others and the way others perceive us. For example, some cultures support an individualistic lifestyle, while others are communal. If, as a team member, you expect people to operate based on your cultural norms, it can lead to conflict and disappointment on a team.

In limiting the impact of our cultural blind spots, a more realistic approach is to evaluate the rationale behind the expectations that we have of others.

For example, directness is one other factor that varies significantly across cultures. On one end of the spectrum, some cultures do not take kindly to the use of the word 'no' as a response to a request, regardless of how unreasonable that request might be. A more culturally acceptable answer would be, "let me think about it and get back to you."

In other cultures, we see the other end of the spectrum, where a higher value is placed on being abrupt and direct as a sign of respect.

As leaders, we should never forget that our interpretation of someone's behavior is mainly influenced by our own culture. If we have the presence of mind to carefully evaluate the factors that drive our feelings and perceptions in certain cases, we will have a much easier time getting along with others.

The Role of Psychometrics in Building Awareness

For a long time, I was under the misguided impression that I had myself all figured out. It wasn't until I started to experience the feelings of burnout, fatigue, and frustration that it became clear that I was being stretched too far outside of my comfort zone. An important thing to note here is that burnout and frustration are both indicative of some amount of misalignment—never ignore these cues.

We had gotten to a point in our coaching practice where it became necessary to select an assessment tool for our clients. My wife introduced me to Predictive Index as a viable alternative. The partner selection process for PI required that I complete a 6-minute behavioral assessment. At first, I was hesitant to complete it, but my curiosity got the best of me, so I took the test.

It took me between 5-6 minutes to complete the assessment, and I was blown away at the level of accuracy in results. It was nothing short of amazing. It was not just the accuracy that captivated my attention but also the overall experience of going over my results in a one-on-one read-back session.

This journey of self-discovery had a transformative impact on the way I moved forward because it affirmed things I already knew about myself so that I could confidently leverage these behaviors to push ahead.

The results also exposed me to some of my blind spots and areas that I needed to grow in, intentionally. Because it came from an objective source, I had no one to be mad at or to blame for being biased against me. I simply had to own the things I knew and even the things I came to learn about myself. Until you give yourself the gift of awareness, you are truly riding blind. In my experience, I found it to be both empowering and liberating.

Now, I always ask leaders and coaching clients the big question: "Who are you?" or, "Do you truly know what kind of person you are?". I must give credit to The PI Behavioral Assessment® and the role it played in my journey towards self-discovery.

How about you? Do you have a good handle on your strengths and potential blind spots? Suppose you are in a position where you are constantly frustrated or find yourself feeling like you don't belong. In that case, this could mean that there is some misalignment between who you are and the role you are in, the team you are on, the culture of the organization, or your mentorship.

Using psychometric tools, such as The PI Behavioral Assessment, Myers Briggs, DiSC, or even Gallup's Strength Finder can unlock meaningful insights into your personality. A word of caution that I must mention concerning assessment tools is that they are definitely a starting point for a discussion to take place, not the final determining factor on who you are.

These tools are not intended to put people in a box or to determine whether a person is competent enough to take on certain roles. As complex beings, we are also creatures of our environment with abilities that have been shaped by experiences, education, and social exposure. Thus, because I might have a certain result on my assessment, it doesn't mean that I lack the ability to stretch into other areas.

In 2019, our partners at PI conducted a survey of 127,000 respondents with the aim to determine the behavioral make-up of individuals working on a team. From their research, they determined that there are four main categories within which a person's behaviors and preferred work styles are normally manifested on the job.

1. ***Innovation and Agility:*** These individuals tend to be driven by a more creative, innovative, entrepreneurial, and risk-tolerant style. They enjoy opportunities for new product development.

2. ***Teamwork and Employee Experience:*** These individuals tend to build relationships, commitment, and engagement. They prefer activities that will help build a cultivating environment for their teams. They are people-oriented and value meaningful one-on-one connection,

3. ***Process and Precision:*** These individuals tend to maintain stability, predictability, and efficiency. They enjoy taking on business process improvement projects and taking a methodical approach to things.

4. ***Results and Discipline:*** These individuals are focused on productivity, metrics, and competition. They enjoy tracking data such as the Key Performance Indicators (KPI) and other metrics that show how well the

team is performing relative to established goals.[xxiii]

Which of the groups mentioned above would you most likely fit into? Sometimes, we know ourselves to some degree and can make accurate guesses. However, my recommendation is to take the guesswork out of this process when it comes to your self-discovery journey. Use a reputable and trustworthy tool to know and learn about yourself.

John Maxwell talked about three types of people in his book: *The 15 Invaluable Laws of Growth*. One group of people is clueless about what they would like to do—they are just flat-out confused. The other group knows what they need to do, but they fail to do it; this keeps them frustrated. And the final group is the fulfilled group because they are aware of themselves and are actively doing what they need to do.[xxiv]

Along my success journey, I've vacillated between all three groups. I must admit that the moment I embraced the path towards self-awareness and took the steps that aligned with my natural strengths, everything changed.

I would like to share six of the steps I have taken to develop self-awareness.

1. Solicit honest feedback from others (friends, family, and managers).
2. Identify and complete scientific-based behavioral and personal assessments.
3. Be intentional about identifying glows (areas of strength) and growth (potential weaknesses).

4. Establish personal development goals to build on your strengths and limit the impact of your blind spots.
5. Monitor your progress by taking note of actions and behaviors that signal growth or the lack of growth.
6. Allow your faith to be the glue that brings all the steps together.

In addition to taking steps towards self-awareness, what holds more importance is the implementation of some principles in your daily routine to sustain yourself on this journey. Below is what I call my "Daily 4". I strongly recommend you use them:

1. Commit to learning something that will help you to grow daily. For me, it is reading a book, watching helpful videos, or taking an online course.

2. Secure a **network** of support that will assist you in growing in your area of weakness. Expand your circle of friends and associates to include people you would like to emulate.

3. Be intentional about identifying and capitalizing on growth opportunities. It could be a tough relationship with a colleague, a daunting task, or a skill you need to master.

4. Set **goals** and be intentional about achieving them. Having both long-term and short-term goals is crucial. I personally write these down and revisit

them on a weekly or monthly basis.

Reflection Questions: Awareness

- Identify and complete a psychometric assessment using either (PI Behavioral Assessment, DiSC or Myers Briggs) and document some of the strengths and weaknesses identified.

- Meet with three (3) to five (5) people you trust and have a relationship with and ask them to share with you the first strength or blind spots that comes to their mind when they think about you. Write them down.

- What steps will you take moving forward to leverage the strengths identified above?

- What steps will you take moving forward to limit the impact of your potential blind spots?

Chapter Five: Agility

"We cannot become what we need by remaining what we are. Change is inevitable. Growth is optional."
- John C. Maxwell

One of the most fool-proof ways to rank among the list of the extinct is to become complacent with your past or present achievements. Today, businesses are challenged to remain on the cutting edge with product development, technological, and scientific breakthroughs as the solution to emerging problems.

They do this for one reason: to remain relevant. This is also the case for leaders who want to remain at the top of their game. We cannot get there by staying married to what has already been tested and proven. Becoming a leader of agility demands that we maintain a mindset that will consistently lead us towards personal growth and development.

There is an aphorism I have often heard: "If it isn't broke, why fix it?" This question perplexed me as a child. There were several reasons for this, but the main one was, why should we wait until something is broken to fix it? We should always look for new and innovative ways to avoid brokenness, complacency, and mediocrity. To me, this is the essence of agile leadership.

Agile leadership is about embracing a new and innovative mindset that will consistently inspire and influence those around us to grow into the best versions of themselves. Agile leadership is not satisfied with maintaining the status quo. Complacency and stagnancy are nuisances to an agile leader.

One writer describes an agile leader as 'being flexible, adaptable, and fast with decision-making.' Because of agility in leadership, today, we are able to enjoy the convenience of air travel, tunnels below the sea, videoconferencing, and GPS. These discoveries have revolutionized the way we travel, work, communicate and do business.

It is interesting to note that while most people are ready to embrace the results of agility, many are against the mindset and behaviors of agile leaders. One of the greatest innovators the world has ever seen, Bill Gates, opined, "Success today requires the agility and drive to rethink, reinvigorate, react, and reinvent constantly."[xxv] Agile leaders must be willing to take a position that may be unpopular and have the confidence to push through against these oppositions.

In the Absence of Agile Leadership

The dinosaur is said to have been a very powerful predator, yet they have now been relegated to the land of antiquity. Despite their size, power, and hunting skills, they are no longer among us. Sadly, the only presence they have in this world is in museums and tales.

Why did cockroaches make it to the 21st century, and dinosaurs didn't? I believe it is because the cockroach was able to integrate the key tenets of agility as a part of its survival style, a skill that the dinosaurs clearly lacked. Cockroaches have managed to outlive the dinosaur, pesticides, the bottom of shoes, and every other exterminating factor that civilization has thrown at them.

Cockroaches remained innovative, flexible, and adaptable along the way. Because of their adaptability to their constantly changing environments, to this day, they remain one of the most dominant species among living creatures. As gross as they are, there is a whole lot we could learn from a cockroach as leaders.

Financial downturns, increased competition, market disruptions, and talent shortages are all exterminating factors that will challenge our ability to lead and impact a team or organization.

So, which is it? Does a person knowingly choose the fate of the dinosaur? Most of us are not, by nature, self-destructive beings who would (given the opportunity) choose a course that would lead to our own professional extinction. It is safe to assume that most would prefer an outcome that will allow them to remain relevant while expanding their legacy well beyond their time. So, why is this the path less traveled?

People remain on the "Dinosaur Avenue" for the following reasons:

1. They have a false sense of security in their present

position.

2. They fail to believe and accept that things and times will change.
3. They fail to adjust and adapt.

Their unwillingness to remain open-minded and flexible in the face of a changing landscape deprives them of opportunities that could change the trajectory of their lives for the better.

We have seen this approach repeatedly in our offices, families, relationships, businesses, and sadly in our own leadership. There is always a miserable ending to this path.

One of the best definitions of leadership that I have heard is from John Maxwell, and within this context, it is worth repeating: "Leadership is influence, nothing more, nothing less.[xxvi]" If you are a leader and you have lost the ability to influence your team, it means that it is time for you to relinquish your role and find another one. Those you lead look to you for a sense of direction, to be inspired, and work towards realizing the vision you have laid out.

When you can no longer inspire or motivate your team to see the big picture or to think beyond the here and now, you will lose your ability to influence or impact them. Imagine sitting at a lunch meeting with someone pitching a VCR business to you. They are soliciting your investment, claiming that this business holds lucrative promise. Would you invest your hard-earned cash in a

VCR business because it might be lucrative?

There is a high chance that you would refer them to one of the best museums around. Relevance is as crucial to your leadership as eating is to our existence. It is important for your team to witness and experience your presence and relevance to growing. It should be done in such a way that your absence leaves a significant void.

We must be cognizant of the fact that we can be on the right road but headed in the wrong direction. My advice to you is to stay off Dinosaur Avenue. Choose the path less traveled. Resist the urge to maintain the status quo. When it comes to agility, there are three important words that I want you to use as your north star: Success, Relevance, and Influence. Agility becomes much easier once these three factors are at the forefront of your mind.

Overcoming Fears

Few things can have a more paralyzing effect on your leadership than the fear of uncertainty. The proven way always seems to be more accessible.

Once a process or method has been etched deep within our subconscious as something, which is celebrated by those we admire, it becomes difficult for us to choose a different path. While it is not the worst decision you could possibly make, it is a safe one, and sometimes, the safest decision is not necessarily what's best for our career and leadership.

Based on the interviews and interactions with executive coaching clients, here are three popular fear factors that serve as a deterrent to agile leadership:

1. Fear of losing support.
2. Fear of failure.
3. Fear of being different.

People who refuse to embrace or accommodate your agile approach are the ones who will celebrate the rewards when they recognize the benefits. I often ask those who face similar struggles, "Are you going to allow the opinion of others to prevent you from being successful?"

Everyone has an opinion, and it is their unassailable right to share what they think. You should never view feedback for anything more than what it truly is. It is merely an opinion. You must seek assurance from the fact that the success of your goals is not directly linked to its popularity.

Ditch the Plan—Embrace Your Purpose

Susan David has produced some very interesting concepts concerning emotional agility. I believe emotional agility to be a very useful and important aspect of agile leadership. In her book, "Emotional Agility," she emphasizes the need to unhook and embrace change so that we can thrive in our careers and life in general[xxvii].

In one of the stories Susan mentions the tale of a captain aboard a British battleship, who was "making routine maneuvers on rough seas to get back to shore". The captain, who was worried about the deteriorating weather conditions, stayed on the ship's bridge to keep an eye on what was going on.

One night, the lookout on the bridge alerted the captain about a light on the starboard bow.

"Is it stationary or moving astern?" the captain asked.

In response to the question by the captain, the lookout responded in the affirmative. Alarmed by the news, the captain recognized what it meant. The battleship was facing the risk of collision with another vessel. The captain immediately ordered his signalman to signal to the ship, "We are on a collision course. I advise you to change course 20 degrees east."

Shortly after, a response came back from the other ship, "You change course 20 degrees west". The captain became quite agitated by the audacity and arrogance of the response. He then asked his signalman to shoot out another message, "I am a captain. You change course 20 degrees east."

In very short order, back came the second response, "I am a second-class seaman. You had still better change course 20 degrees west."

The captain was furious on this occasion. He shouted to the signalman to send back a final message, which highlighted all his credentials along with the rank of his battalion and reiterated his orders. "Change course 20 degrees east right now!". A response came back in a flash, "I am a lighthouse."

This story serves as a reminder of the imminent dangers present when tenured leadership, positional power, and ego gets in the way of having an openness to learn something new and adjusting our style to ensure that we are positioning ourselves for success. This lighthouse is like certain crises or roadblocks that we will face as leaders. No matter how we come at it, the lighthouse cannot change its course. We are the ones who must change our course to avoid the devastating impact of our extinction.

We must be the ones exercising an openness to the fact that sometimes our plans may be rock solid. Also, we might have invested a considerable amount of time and resources into the materialization of the plan. We might even have received raving reviews about how thorough the plans were. But the plan is not our North Star; our North Star is our purpose.

Here is a principle on which I want you to marinate. Regardless of how great we feel about our plans or strategies, we should never allow ourselves to become more loyal to a plan than we are to our purpose. The sea captain's purpose was to safely navigate this ship to the shore. Going on an ego trip with a second-class seaman placed his entire ship, along with all the souls on board, at risk.

Earlier in this book, we addressed awareness and the role it plays in allowing us to deepen our understanding of our strengths and potential blind spots. Our awareness of our purpose and passion should be the driving forces behind our decision-making process.

Our plan might be the map, but our purpose is the

compass. Once we have formed a clear understanding of this, we will be well on our way to becoming agile leaders. The real struggle most leaders face is that they are not able to ditch their plan when it is appropriate to do so and embrace their purpose.

If you treat your purpose as your compass, you will be able to conveniently change the route because your focus will be fixed on the destination. Do not get me wrong, a plan is an important part of the process. Without a plan, we would be wandering aimlessly through our lives and careers, swayed by every wind of change that comes our way. Loyalty to purpose is the one thing that will help us remain anchored as we go along our success journey.

How Do You Become an Agile Leader?

Agility is a concept that was borrowed from the field of project management. It is a contemporary but innovative approach that emphasizes an iterative process that delivers a working deliverable at the end of each project sprint(pre-determined period spanning a week or two). This approach is governed by the agile manifesto which champions four important principles:

1. Individual interactions should be elevated above processes and tools

2. Working deliverable must be elevated above comprehensive documentation

3. Customer collaboration must be made the priority over contract negotiation

4. Responding to change must be prioritized over following a plan.

What does this all mean within the context of leadership, and how can one become a leader of agility? Becoming a leader of agility fundamentally requires leadership that will inspire their team to reflect on how to be more effective, then adapt their style and approach to successfully meet the needs of their clients.

I would like to share five simple steps I've practiced over the years that have yielded me much success.

1. Embrace creativity wherever it may be found, both in yourself and others.
2. Encourage creative tension and differences of opinion.
3. Remain purposeful in your decision-making.
4. Remain curious and adaptable.
5. Embrace and Evaluate Change

Embracing Creativity

Many people are hesitant to embrace creativity. Primarily, it is due to two reasons—the fear of being labeled as different forces us to hide our creative genius. The second reason is that we can become so locked into our preferred way of doing things that there comes the point where we are unwilling to accept the creativity of others. Acknowledging other people's ideas and creativity opens the door to a plethora of possibilities that could bring life-changing results.

Encouraging Creative Tension

One of the biggest advantages of what I do in my consulting business is that I have spent a lot of time learning about the various aspects that influence human behavior. One of these elements that I find the most intriguing is the dominance drive, which accounts for the degree to which some leaders are interested in influencing and impacting their environment.

Those who are higher along the spectrum are likely to act more assertively and independently and deal with confrontation and conflict in a meaningful way. Those lower along the spectrum tend to be more collaborative and supportive but are terrified of conflict and confrontation. Understanding our natural behavioral drives can help us in identifying the specific factors that make us more ambivalent towards conflict and creativity.

There is a concept called *creative tension*. Leadership and team development experts often reference it dealing with conflict amongst team members. It is frequently used to describe the clash of ideas and differences, which sounds like a fight to the undiscerning passerby. When a leader is comfortable enough to allow members of their team to engage in meaningful debates about issues, and at the end, everyone comes away with meaningful solutions, it signifies their agility as leaders. Sometimes, our teams must fight it out. I believe this practice should be acceptable if the fight is strictly reserved for the issue at hand, not out of personal grudges amongst the teammates.

Encouraging collaboration on this level is an

admission that we do not know everything. It is also an opportunity for us to be exposed to other like-minded people or individuals whose differences of opinion and involvement can serve to strengthen our confidence in the decisions we make.

Remain Purposeful and Act Urgently with Decision - making

There are many leaders who allow paralysis by analysis to prevent them from making decisions. Once you have allowed your team to engage in creative tension or debates about the solutions, you should be prepared to make the final decision. On the organizational level, this should be driven by the organization's core values. However, on a personal level, your purpose should be the primary driver.

Remaining Curious and Adaptable

When we remain curious and adaptable, we secure our spot at the cutting edge. Those who fail to stay curious and adaptable experience the reverse. Their unwillingness to remain agile is rooted in fear of the uncertainty and possibly, the pain that awaits them.

I have deliberately used the word pain because sometimes, the way forward, especially in new territories, brings with it its fair share of woe and discomfort. However, pain isn't always bad. The pain of childbirth is a rite of passage to new life. The pain from a broken bone makes us aware that something is wrong and requires medical attention.

The pain from a loss reminds us of our humanity and our innate yearning for healing and support. Our goal should never be to avoid pain; it is to fulfill our purpose. If the pain is what will breathe new life into that project or product—embrace the pain. Never lose your curiosity because of the fear of pain and uncertainty. Never miss an opportunity to adapt to the changing landscape that could lead you to a path of success and new beginnings.

Are you willing to give up your comfort zone to experience your transformation? The Reggae artist, Buju Banton, in one of his songs on his album "Til Shiloh," said, "It's not an easy road when you see the glamor and the glitter, and you think a bed of roses." I hope you have seen this persistent theme throughout each principle I have shared so far. The path less traveled may be paved with a painful experience, but we should never allow this to prevent us from fulfilling our purpose.

Embrace and Evaluate Change

Taking on new frontiers requires adaptability, but you must evaluate the necessity and need for change. Not all changes are good, and as an agile leader, you will have to critically evaluate some changes while embracing others. The rule of thumb is to not change the goal, simply for the sake of doing something new or different. Sometimes it is reasonable to be a skeptic. If the pursued changes do not align with your goals, vision, or plan, it may not be worth embracing.

Benefits of Being an Agile Leader

Before they started to make luxury cars, BMW made

plane engines. Their journey to becoming one of the most prominent forces in the automotive industry was paved with agility at every turn. At one point, they were even making kitchen utensils to keep business afloat.

Some may question whether the intentional effort required to maintain agility is worth it. Some may wonder if they might be better off sticking to the "what-was" which they inherited in terms of practices, policies, plans, and traditions.

Earlier, I spoke about the benefits of an agile approach in project management, and in this section, I want us to focus on the real benefits that one can expect from being an agile leader:

1. It produces highly engaged and responsive employees and team members.
2. It develops high levels of enthusiasm for the most challenging activities.
3. It builds openness and collaboration among members of a team and organization.
4. It inspires confidence not just in you but also in others through capacity building.
5. It helps to secure a strong and stable future for the organization.

If one of your goals is to become a person of influence while experiencing growth and transformation, agility is the key to attaining this objective.

Five Key Drivers for Agile leadership:

As we gloss over some of the major benefits of agile

leadership, it is also essential for us to consider some of the factors that will drive this leadership style. While it gives leaders the competitive edge and relevance required to succeed, there are certain factors that must be present to increase the odds of maintaining agility. Following are the factors which must be present.

1. Integrity
2. Innovation
3. Urgency
4. Engagement
5. Direction

These five drivers help you cultivate a clear, assertive, and decisive mindset, which will empower you beyond the noise and distractions that often limit people to average ways of approaching challenges and opportunities.

Integrity (Accountability)

Oprah Winfrey once said, "Real integrity is doing the right thing, knowing that nobody's going to know whether you did it or not."[xxviii] I recall a conversation with a good friend of mine, Dr. Marcellus Robinson. I was getting ready to take on a new role in a community that would have proven to be a challenge. He gave me a few words of advice, but he made a statement that I believe to be worth repeating. "Jaymie, whenever you lose your integrity as a leader, it is time to call the moving truck."

While it is important to maintain agility in leadership, we must act in a way that allows us to maintain our credibility. We should not risk anything that will compromise that. Authentic leadership is founded on reliability, trust, values, and principles. People trust and follow those who have integrity.

Innovation (Curious and Experimental)

Agile leaders are innovative. They get a real kick out of being the first to do something. They leverage their curiosity to unearth new ideas and develop a safe space for creativity, learning, and consistent growth.

Urgency (Focused and Decisive)

I have missed many opportunities due to my unwillingness to make decisions or act on limited information. I was consumed with getting it all right the first time and not having to deal with any form of failure. As I learned more about agile leadership and the need to be innovative, I realized that agile leaders embrace the value of urgency and being decisive. I also realized that you do not need to have all the ducks in a row to move on with your ideas or plans.

My friend Noel Reid, an entrepreneur, is the epitome of urgency and making big decisions with limited information. I have seen him fail, but always bagging big wins. Interestingly, I have never found him in a state of regret. Whenever I am making any major business moves, I consult him. The reason is that he understands the power of being focused and urgent at the same time. I consider my close friend to be a successful entrepreneur, and I think the secret to his exemplary performance as a business leader is because he does not hesitate to act.

Engagement (Inclusive and Collaborative)

Agile Leaders thrive on engagement. They consider it

their responsibility to create engagement wherever they find an opportunity. Agile leaders understand that engagement creates relationships, and relationships produce results and camaraderie.

A person who embraces agility recognizes the need to be inclusive and collaborative. They understand the power behind joining forces with others. They are conscious that greatness lies in the coming together of different people, who use their differences to create change and impact each other. Many people fail in their businesses, not because their ideas weren't great, but because they lacked key outside perspectives that would have filled the gaps.

Direction (Communicative and Empowering)

When you embrace agility, you become aware of the significance of moving and growing, and where there is a lack of clarity, your job is to provide it.

Agility helps us create direction for our organization, family, teams, and ourselves. We don't cower in the face of roadblocks or hurdles. Instead, we are motivated to remove anything that will prevent us from positively impacting our journey and the journey of those who we lead and serve. As we forge ahead, let us embrace this mindset.

Strategy for Agile Leadership

Leap or Leash Leadership is a concept I developed very early in my leadership journey, mainly through personal observations and research. Remember we spoke earlier about tendencies? As leaders, we all have a particular bent towards being a leap or leash leader.

I can recall an encounter I had while growing up with my neighbor's ferocious dog. This dog was infamous for attacking and biting people, especially children. Just the sound of his growling, and I would become paralyzed with fear. I wanted to run, but my knees betrayed me. My small frame could barely withstand an attack from this dog. What must I do?

Then I heard it, like music to my ears, the sound of his chain reverberating from contact with the rocks below. It was a chained dog. He was tied to a tree in my neighbor's yard and could only go the distance his restraint would allow. At that moment, all he did was bark without a bite. Many leaders operate like they are chained. They are chained to trees of fear, failure, culture, past wins, and their current obstacles. This group of leaders is what I refer to as leash leaders.

Leap and Leash Leaders operate on very opposite ends of the spectrum. Refer below to Table 1.0 for the specific characteristics of a Leap or Leash Leader. Reflect on these characteristics to determine whether you have a tendency towards that of an agile leader bent towards leap leadership or leash leadership.

Leap Leadership Versus Leash Leadership

Leash Leaders	Leap Leaders
Investing all trust in past or proven success	Choosing the best path forward
Guided by plans, rules, and procedures	Guided by purpose
Avoid risks	Take calculated risks
Crippled and deflated by failure	Use failure to one's advantage
Need all the facts to advance	Build and adjust to success
Tied to legacy	Creates and expands legacy

Leap leaders are willing to go beyond their comfort zone, even if this path exposes them to their weaknesses. They indulge in self-discovery that could also reveal their strengths. Leap leaders may face defeat and rejection, but they also tend to manifest higher levels of grit and resilience in the face of setbacks.

Leap leaders have scars because of failures, but their wisdom and experience empower them to take on greater obstacles and secure tremendous wins. Leashed leaders are satisfied with their inheritance and are committed to preserving past achievements but are reluctant to expand. Leashed leaders are tied to legacy and rituals, resulting in which they become unwilling to adjust most of the time. Today I challenge you to take the leap into your next breakthrough and become a leader of agility.

Reflection Question: Agility

- Describe an experience you had, when you had to make significant changes mid-way a plan, project or idea. Was this easy for you to do? Write down the reasons for your answer.

- Based on what you've read, would agility help you to be more effective as a leader? If so, what adjustments are you willing to make moving forward.

- Review the characteristics of a Leap or Leashed leader, which of these traits best describe you?

- How will you incorporate agility as part of your leadership style moving forward?

Chapter Six: Clarity

"More important than the quest for certainty is the quest for clarity." – Francois Gautier

Amidst all the fog and uncertainty life throws at us, there exists a lens which, when fully engaged, can lead to fulfillment, transformation, and the success we seek— it's called clarity.

Numerous organizations, teams, and families have successfully incorporated this principle to bring a new sense of meaning and direction to the way they act. Clarity has inspired the confidence of many and has had a profound impact on business outcomes.

I have always been intrigued by the Nike slogan: "Just Do It." It sparks a sense of action and urgency in my mind. However, for Nike to have attained its success in the sports apparel industry, it must have invested a significant amount of time and resources in gaining clarity on its vision, mission, and core values—they are doing "it."

In one of my recent *Strategic Alignment* podcasts, Jay Moore, a financial coach, and mentor of mine, commented on people who engage in the fruitless act of spinning wheels. The major reason for doing it is to get a kick out of telling friends how busy they are.

When it becomes evident that they were just spinning wheels, it leads to feelings of frustration and a lack of fulfillment.

I recall the first time my wife and I sat down for our first meeting around the strategies we would put in place for our consulting practice to grow. We used some of the things that I considered to be cliched, such as vision boards and mind mapping, to help bring clarity to our messaging. It was a frustrating process, and it took us a couple of tries to successfully devise a plan.

Coming out of those meetings, I felt a deep sense of fulfillment. From the joy evident on my face, one would think I had already achieved the goals we laid out in those discussions. Comparing the way, I felt before and how I felt at the end of the process was like night and day. Before we started the process, I know we were on the right highway, but I was uncertain if we were heading in the right direction.

I am reminded of my move from Salem West Virginia to Pottstown Pennsylvania. I had printed all my directions from MapQuest but for some strange reason I was not as attentive as I should have been when reading the directions and as a result, I spent an extra hour on the right highway but heading in the wrong direction. So often we have good intentions and motivation but for some reason we get lost in the weeds or we end up majoring in the minor things and minoring in the things that are most important.

What is Clarity?

I love Pat Lencioni's books on leadership and team development. My personal favorite is the *Four Obsessions of an Extraordinary Executive*. In this book, Pat brilliantly uses a leadership fable to document the myriad successes leaders can glean, both at the personal and team level, from leveraging the key tenets of clarity[xxix].

The main character in the fable - Rich, gave his team the gift of clarity. Through this one act, his team made clear and concise decisions, had more spirited discussions during meetings, and secured the results they had been seeking (Lencioni). Rich used a simple system as part of his hiring process to help ensure that all senior-level executives received a complete and comprehensive orientation into the organizational culture and expectations.

At the organizational level, clarity is achieved when employees clearly understand the company's overall vision, mission, and core values. On the personal level, clarity is achieved when someone has a deep understanding of who they are, what they hope to achieve, and how they will accomplish this (Jennifer Olney)[xxx]. Success is well within reach when we can merge both personal and organizational clarity.

Clarity is that one factor that could turn what others may view as parochial roads into highways. It turns dreams into full-blown reality, hobbies into a thriving business, and experiments into solutions. Without clarity, you run the risk of taking on someone else's journey, accomplishing someone else's goals, and fulfilling someone else's dream.

What if I should ask you to share your purpose with me? Would the answer be something that you could easily articulate without hesitation?

If you find yourself among the few individuals who can answer this question with ease, then you are much further along your success journey than most.

In my line of work, I have had the pleasure of interacting with people from different walks of life. During my interactions, I have observed that people answer with much greater ease the questions related to what they do as a job, more so than they can articulate their purpose and goals.

This information is expressed with great ease because it happens to be what they spend most of their time 'doing.' Rather than seeking clarity about their identity, some people align their identities with what they do.

When it comes to our purpose, goals, and aspirations, a successful career or employment is not a substitute for clarity. Clarity is the key success factor that will help you realize what you want to achieve and provide you with a clear path to get there. It is the embodiment of what drives you, your passion, your purpose, and your goals.

What happens in the Absence of Clarity?

No one wants to wander aimlessly through life, with little to show for the time and hard work they've invested in the actions they took. With clarity, we have a map that can help us learn which steps to take to achieve our goals.

Steve Maraboli – the best-selling author and coach, makes one of the most cogent statements on what to expect in the absence of clarity: "It's a lack of clarity that creates chaos and frustration. Those emotions are poison to any living goal."[xxxi]

Seeking personal growth and development without clarity is tantamount to driving blindly during peak-hour traffic. When we walk blindly, our only resort is to depend on others to lead us to our destination. It is not my intention to imply that we should not submit to the leadership of others; however, sometimes, this submission comes at the expense of us having to settle with less than what our potential allows.

When our submission to the leadership of others comes because of clarity, we are far more likely to reach the destination we had initially set out to achieve. Holding a clear understanding of what needs to get done gives rise to a sense of confidence that we are being led in the right direction.

Is your current path leading you in the right direction? With each waking moment, can you honestly feel a sense of reassurance that the daily actions you are taking are leading you towards your goal? Or do you experience a constant unease every day from the things you spend most of your day doing?

If your answers to these questions evokes feelings of frustration, then you would have taken the first step towards achieving clarity by realizing its lack thereof. Neal

Ramon suggests that in the absence of clarity, one can anticipate;

1. Confusion and mental turmoil
2. Poor performance
3. Delays in the achievement of goals
4. Lack of efficiency
5. Frustration, stress and overwhelm[xxxii]

Each of these factors will result in low productivity and ineffective leadership. Confusion has a very negative impact on decision-making. One of the most frustrating feelings is working with a team where people are unclear about their roles and contributions. On the personal level, lack of clarity prevents us from operating at our optimum because we are unable to evaluate when we are performing at our best.

Knowing who you are and what you are working towards allows you to determine the best steps to take, the best team to assemble, and the best tools to use to get you the results you seek.

Clarity allows you to be efficient. In underscoring the difference between productivity and efficiency, Jessica Greene provides a definition for efficiency that captures clarity's effect on a person or organization. She says that whereas productivity measures how much you produce over a period, efficiency on the other hand, is all about being productive with less effort.

Rick Warren, in his book, *The Purpose Driven Life*, writes: "Without a clear purpose, you have no foundation on which to base your decisions, allocate your time, and use your resources. You will tend to make choices based on circumstances, pressures, and your mood at that moment."[xxxiii]

In achieving our goals, we do not necessarily need certainty as much as clarity. When clarity is present, we waste less time, are more productive, and allow our purpose to drive our success. In the absence of clarity, we face a plethora of challenges with decision-making, selecting the right team, cultivating the right habits, and capitalizing on the best opportunities.

A Leader of Clarity

When it comes to leaders of clarity, the success stories are many. However, few of these leaders rank in the same league as the great Dr. Martin Luther King Jr. King, whose vision, purpose, and mission were borderline prophetic.

"We have the attitude of love, the method of passive resistance, and we believe that violence is self-defeating. If you live by the sword, you will die by the sword," said Martin Luther King JR.

His famous speech during the march on Washington and his last speech also captured the very essence of clarity. The vision of this giant and futurist is still relevant today. From his advocacy for civil rights to his personal approach, one can attest to the fact that clarity of purpose was a permanent fixture in his life.

Dr. King's courage in the face of hate and discrimination signaled an unwavering commitment to his calling. He was young, intelligent, and black. During the 1960s, as the United States of America struggled to surmount a crisis brought about because of poor race relations (specifically against African Americans), his leadership helped turn the tides in favor of African-Americans and other underserved communities.

In his pursuit for justice and equality, Dr. King was clear on a few things. The first thing was the extent of the problem he faced. He was aware of the pervasiveness of systemic racism. He was also conscious of the widespread opposition from without and within the civil rights movement for his messaging around a non-violent stance against racial violence.

Not only was he aware of the adversity he faced, but he was also aware of his gift as a transformational leader, speaker, motivator, and intellect, which allowed him to remain unshakeable. Armed with his clarity of purpose, Dr. King was willing to stand up for his race, even if it meant he would have to endure abuse, hardships, imprisonment, and threats to his life.

Dr. King's clarity of purpose, passion, vision, and the need for change were evident. His influence and impact continue to reverberate around the world to this day. Through this clarity, he was able to inspire, motivate, and give hope to millions.

The question may arise: what motivated Martin Luther King and inspired him to lead a civil rights movement in the face of death threats and mounting danger? James Clear has provided us with the best answer in his book, *Atomic Habits*, "Many people think they lack motivation when what they really lack is clarity."[xxxiv]

Dr. Martin Luther King was clear about his purpose and vision for equality. The urge to eliminate social vices was what fueled him to move forward. It was the reason why he courageously confronted the discrimination, hatred, and segregation and was a source of motivation for many other civil rights activists.

As I reflect on the life and legacy of Dr. King, it's evident that clarity can be frightening. Clarity exposes you to the realities of your journey and the fact that you may not have all that it takes to individually handle certain challenges. Clarity empowers you to see the good and the bad ahead of you. It allows you to confront the potential challenges and failures that you are destined to encounter.

Too often we see talented leaders and athletes fail to generate the impact commensurate with their talent. Dr. King recognized through clarity that despite being a talented speaker, leader, and civil rights activist he needed the support of the masses to get his message across to those in power. His unconventional nonviolent approach to violence was laughed at by many but proved to be the best path that could have been taken.

Levels of Clarity

I was in the throes of working on a presentation for a group of executives on clarity when I came across an article written by Garry Wood[xxxv]. In this article, he addressed the three levels of clarity. They are absolute truths, objective facts, and assumptions. I would dare to add another level, which is limitations. I view absolute truth as unchangeable realities, the things you cannot change about yourself.

Absolute truths are things that don't every change. This represents some characteristics you inherited at birth, while some are based on decisions made for you. Examples include your race, parents, place of birth, date of birth, and natural gifts. Acknowledging your unchangeable reality is one of the most critical steps in achieving clarity.

Are there some absolute truths about you that you are ashamed to own? Do you wish you could change them? Do you feel less of a person when you think about your unchangeable realities? Reflecting on these questions is a crucial first step in embracing who you are and securing the support you need to move forward unapologetically.

According to Woods, objective facts are those things that are verifiable and can be proven. Acknowledgment of objective facts is essential to gaining the trust and confidence of others. Such attributes can either help you move forward or serve as a hurdle in your path. We operate in communities, and it takes a community to achieve sustainable success collectively while doing several things independently.

The third level of clarity has to do with assumptions. It has to do with assumptions we form based on what we perceive to be the truth. The clear distinction is that this assumption is not necessarily based on any fact.

Oftentimes, we are presumptuous about the things we don't know, and this becomes our biggest mistake.

Whenever we give way to this mindset, missed opportunities become a habit. Have you ever assumed that you were underqualified for a position within an organization, only to discover that someone with far less qualification was selected for the role? To add salt to your wounds, the person appointed for the said role consults you for advice on this new assignment.

Three Types of People in Relation to Clarity

In her book, *Clarity*, Karen Martin came up with three different categories of people when it comes on to clarity: Clarity Avoiders, Clarity Pursuers, and Clarity Blind. As we explore the three categories in the following section, I invite you to reflect on which of these categories resonates with your personality[xxxvi].

Clarity Avoiders

These people are either over-satisfied with their limited view on life or are unwilling to adjust. Adapting and making changes will take them too far outside their comfort zones. Their lived experience is like pond creatures who will never experience the incredible adventures of the vast ocean. Clarity avoiders are willing to live in ignorance, even after realizing the adverse impacts of their ignorance on their growth.

While preparing for a mid-semester exam, I was required to read five chapters. I read four. I felt that my grasp of the content from the four chapters I had covered would be sufficient to help me secure at least a passing grade. If there are questions on the next chapter, my thought was that I could ad-lib my way through. Unfortunately, luck decided to ditch me that day.

On test day, a good portion of the questions was from the chapter I did not study. My performance on the exam was beyond poor. I was devastated. Moliere shared an important piece of information; "It is not only what we do, but also what we do not do, for which we are accountable."[xxxvii] Deciding not to read that chapter so I could be in the most prepared position was a lazy cop-out. Deciding to avoid something does not serve as an escape route for the consequences you will face for not doing it.

When working in a team or participating in meetings, you will find that the clarity avoiders are poised to shut down new perspectives or insights that challenges groupthink. These people celebrate mediocrity and always have an excuse in their arsenal to unleash in the face of sub-par performance.

Clarity avoiders live in a state of ambiguity. One way to know if this is where you live is to evaluate the quality of results you are experiencing, whether personally or as a leader, and ask yourself: Am I a clarity avoider?

Clarity Pursuers

When I think about **Clarity Pursuers**, the first person who comes to my mind is my friend Luigi Allen. I have never seen Luigi set a goal that he has failed to achieve. Luigi loves learning, and he is not afraid of diving into new information, even if it comes at the cost of exposure to his weaknesses.

Luigi's love for information and his passion for pursuing clarity has led him to experience monumental success. His journey of success started on the streets of Jamaica, as he associated with gangs, getting in and out of trouble. Today, his success spans multiple degrees, high-level certifications, and he's now a sorted-after leader in one of the world's leading Fortune 500 corporations.

Clarity pursuers are not afraid of embracing the new information because they understand that commensurate with the new challenges and opportunities is a chance to grow personally and professionally. Clarity pursuers are not floaters who only enjoy the surface. They take an interest in diving deep and wide. They wholeheartedly embrace curiosity.

Clarity Blind

Some leaders who read the daily papers or watch the daily news remain on the cutting edge when it comes to new tools within their respective industries. Although they are fixated on consuming new information at every turn, it doesn't seem to bring any change.

These individuals are **clarity blind**. It means that they make the wrong decisions with the right information. The real challenge is to help a person who is clarity blind. I say challenge because even if you suggest a solution, it may not be helpful to them since they will not make the decision to change. It is important to avoid becoming a "clarity blind" person at all costs. To achieve this, we must evaluate the information we receive. Furthermore, we must not hold ourselves back but rather move ahead and seize the opportunities. If there is an opportunity to improve our lives and leadership, we should make the most of it.

Roadblocks to Clarity

Roadblocks make for an exciting success journey. It may just be the satisfaction one feels from surmounting the challenges and getting back on track. To experience this ecstatic feeling, you must identify these roadblocks to overcome them successfully. The barriers related to clarity that I have discovered throughout my journey are worth mentioning. The major roadblocks to clarity include arrogance, conscious and unconscious biases, lack of curiosity, and the fear of the unknown.

Leo Tolstoy said, "An arrogant person considers himself perfect. It is the chief harm of arrogance. It interferes with a person's main task in life – becoming a better person."[xxxviii] Believing that your current position or state is the best, with no need to aim for better, can harm your growth and success.

Arrogance has a way of turning a business that was once booming into a distant memory. A positive self-image is a good thing, but there is an inherent danger in holding a resistant mindset to growth, improvement, and expansion. Settling for where we are with no intentions of adjusting, adapting, or rethinking our way forward is a recipe for expiration.

It is like that senior high school basketball player who no longer sees the need to attend practices because he dominates the sport. He spends no time going over the game, replays, or listening to his coach.

Then, when he finally makes it to college and spends his first two seasons on the bench, he becomes disappointed. Because the only help he got from his arrogance was a lid. This lid impeded his ability to evolve into the best version of himself. Take it from me, if you are to give yourself a gift, you do not want the gift of a lid.

The second roadblock to clarity is our personal biases. Often, we become stuck because of certain preferences that hold us hostage. Our prejudices prevent us from perceiving things in a fair way. It causes us to discriminate against things that do not align with our preferences.

We fail to discern between a great opportunity and an average possibility when we fail to see clearly through the fog of our preferences. The key to overcoming this obstacle is to remain open-minded when it comes to our differences. Embracing meaningful difference is one of the secrets behind successful leaders. Being objective and open to the truth means not assuming that familiarity, comfort, and generally accepted ways of thinking are synonymous with being right.

One of the most prominent manifestations of the negative impact that personal biases can have on clarity is in the process of hiring. Senior executive roles within organizations are the most consequential hiring decisions regarding the organizational culture and performance.

We miss opportunities to hire the right people in key roles when we allow personal biases to be the barometer through which we measure job fit. When clarity is present, hiring decisions will be easier by reducing the complexity and ambiguity around what to look for. This decision will be driven by the core values, job requirements, behavioral and cultural alignment, rather than intuition.

Clarity and Curiosity

Most of the great discoveries and breakthroughs we celebrate today were only made possible because someone was curious enough to explore the unknown. Today's most successful leaders within the leadership landscape, such as Elon Musk, Bill Gates, and Mark Zuckerberg, have credited curiosity for their success. Their decision to remain curious has given birth to revolutionary breakthroughs in the way we work, travel, communicate and shop.

When we fail to embrace an inquisitive mindset, we are closing off several windows of opportunities and preventing ourselves from seeing what lies beyond a confusing yet exciting journey. Lack of curiosity keeps us from seeing the next move of our competition or remaining on the cutting edge for new and emerging trends that could set us up for our next big break. In an article, *Why Curiosity Matters* in Harvard Business Review, it is proposed that "When our curiosity is triggered, we tend to think more deeply and rationally about decisions and can then come up with more creative solutions."[xxxix]

What are the Benefits of Clarity?

So far, we've explored what happens in the absence of clarity, but here we will delve into some of the benefits of clarity:

1. Set clear priorities
2. Build our self-confidence
3. Have a sense of direction
4. Secure transformation
5. Eliminate distractions

Clarity allows you to set clear priorities. When you have your priorities right sided up, you can invest the time, effort, and resources into the areas that are most relevant to attaining your goals and remaining true to your purpose. Having priorities allows you to stay focused on your next step, opportunities, and the inevitable challenges that you will encounter.

Clear priorities also help you detect distractions, as it keeps you more focused, and your goal lies clear in front of you. Most of the time, distraction takes root in the absence of clearly defined priorities.

My grandparents would tell us that the devil finds work for idle hands as a child. Those people who are focused on their priorities are less likely to get caught up with distractions, which could detract them from their purpose. Remaining focused allows you to make the critical moves and paves a straightforward way to your destination—one step at a time.

Clarity allows you to approach life and leadership with confidence. When you are aware of yourself, your goals, and your approach, you gain a sense of certainty about yourself that is not easily extinguished.

When clarity is present, it becomes easier to execute

better job interviews, give the best of work presentations, contribute effectively to discussions, and explicitly convey your message and ideas. In the next chapter, we will delve more deeply into confidence, so you can unlock the secrets on how to lead your team and organization confidently towards success.

Clarity gives direction. With clarity, you are not confused about the path you need to take as you pursue your goals. With clarity, even the most complex and ambiguous problems become solvable. It allows you to navigate ambiguity with assertiveness. Give me a manager who provides clarity to their team, and I will give you a team of high performers.

Clarity is transformational. In recent times, the NeuroLeadership Institute worked with the leadership of Microsoft to provide their employees with clarity on the key competencies that would transform the culture of the organization. The three factors mentioned were: creating clarity, generating energy, and delivering success. Take note that the first step along this journey is to create clarity.[xl]

If we want your team, organization, or network to embrace change, the number one thing you must have in your arsenal is clarity on a personal level. It is then that we should provide clarity to the team and organization.

Steps to clarity – 'What', 'Why' and 'How'

"Think of clarity as the fuel of vision and action. If you aren't clear about the 'why and how' you will never lift your vision off the ground (Jennifer Olney).[xli] When you know what you want, why you want it and how you can achieve it, you have achieved clarity.

Whenever I am asked to explain the granular aspects of clarity, I take no reservations in doing so. I believe that when a person has fully grasped the 'what' the 'why' and the 'how' they can confidently take action and make decisions. Too often we see people who work hard fail to reap the benefits of their efforts because they are being swayed by every wind of new discoveries that comes along.

Finding your *"what"* requires careful examination of personal goals, ideas, habits, or behaviors you seek to achieve, modify or rid yourself of. Your 'why' is your reason for pursuing a given goal. And the 'how' addresses how you will pursue your goals.

Consider the case of Shelly-Ann. She recently graduated from college. Her Master's degree is in Human Resources Management. Straight out of college she was offered an internship to work as an accounting clerk at an accounting firm owned by her father's friend. The pay was tolerable for a recent college graduate with no experience, and she had not heard from the other places she had applied to.

As Shelly-Ann mulled over her decision, she sought to apply the three main tenets of clarity to help make up her mind. As she reviewed some of the goals she had after graduation, one of the most important goals for her, was landing in a junior Human Resource role that would help her to build experience in her area of specialty. Through this process, Shelly was able to uncover both her 'what' and 'why'.

She started to explore job boards and reached out directly to Human Resource Departments and recruiters. After two weeks of trying, she landed some interviews. Shelly-Ann found out her 'how' and was able to stay the course and not deviate due to the convenience of just landing a paycheck.

There are many people whose careers have been sidetracked because of the absence of clarity. We should be very intentional about determining what we want, why we want it and take steps to go after this.

Reflection Questions: Clarity

- Take a moment to reflect on a time when you struggled with a lack of clarity in a role or organization? How did this impact your productivity level?

- Do you know your purpose in life? Describe how you feel when fully emersed in activities that are aligned with your purpose.

- Do you struggle with any of the following barriers to Clarity and if so, how are they affecting your ability to deliver top results?
    - Lack of curiosity
    - Arrogance
    - Biases
    - Fear

Chapter Seven:
Confidence

With realization of one's own potential and self-confidence in one's ability, one can build a better world." - The Dalai Lama

Confidence is not an elusive element exclusively bestowed based on gender, race, age group, or religious affiliation. Being a confident leader requires you to believe in your own abilities, a willingness to hold people accountable to established standards, and to inspire them to have a psychological commitment to the success of your team and organization.

The ideal way to achieve this as a leader is to show up, fully aware that the spotlight is pointed in your direction, deservedly so. You have every right to be standing where you are. As such you will exude the magnetic effect that pulls people in your direction. People who may not know you but are deciding whether they can trust you and buy into your vision. But what does a confident leader look and sound like?

Floyd Mayweather has taken a lot of heat from the media and critics about his intellectual abilities. Still, I must admit that my fascination with him grew after I watched one of his interviews. When asked about what is behind his drive to win, his response was, "I'm not the sharpest knife in the drawer, but I'm a very sharp knife, and I'm in the drawer."[xlii]

Mayweather is undeniably known for his confidence, both inside and outside of the ring. Because of this, he is feared and respected by his opponents. Statements like the one mentioned earlier leaves very little room for questioning his fifteen major world titles and his undefeated world champion position attained upon his retirement.

One of the mistakes many people make is to compare themselves with all the other "knives in the drawer." They fail to acknowledge what they bring to the table, considering themselves as a less sharp knife in the drawer. Missing out on opportunities to embrace their unique gifts and talents.

To make things worse, many people start to take on a new identity because they forget that they are a 'knife' with their unique edge. This is tantamount to a tamed lion behaving like a domesticated cat. A very sad sight to behold.

You need to come to the realization that you are already in the game; you have what it takes to rise to the occasion. This is why it is important to believe in yourself enough to know that you need not compare yourself to anyone else in order to reach your desired goals.

One of the most fulfilling aspects of being a coach is to witness the transformative impact of unadulterated self-belief. I have had clients who came to me with their self-confidence, buried beneath feelings of inadequacies, insecurities, and low self-esteem and this is mostly attributable to them engaging in the destructive act of comparing themselves to others.

After several coaching sessions, positive reinforcement, and with the help of objective behavioral assessments, they slowly begin to emerge as confident leaders who are fully aware of what they bring to the table.

One of my favorite movies of all time is *The Gladiator*. Russel Crowe puts on an incredible performance as Maximus. Among all the great leadership qualities he exhibits in this movie, I am particularly moved by his confidence on the battlefield, but more so as a slave and prisoner.

His self-confidence inspired the other prisoners. This sparked a revolution against their oppressors, even in the face of pain and hopelessness. A spark of confidence as their shining light was enough to make them victorious, even when all odds were not in their favor.

As you chart your leadership journey, self-belief is critical to your success. However, you also need to be aware of the impact that people's expectations and perceptions can have on your decision-making. Sometimes, their advice or suggestions, whether intended or unintended, may place you in a box if you choose to heed everything that comes your way.

My first job out of college was at a school. Within my first six months on the job as a counselor, I mastered my role and exceeded the expectations of my superiors. My performance was evident from the excellent reviews of my supervisor. The parents' feedback was nothing short of remarkable, and I successfully earned the respect of both my colleagues and students.

After two years of working with the organization, two promotional opportunities became available. I desired a change of roles because I felt that I had outgrown my current position. The opening I had my eye on was a directorship role. When the founder learned that I was interested in that role, he requested a meeting with me.

During the meeting, he discouraged me from applying for the position. I gathered from the discussion that it was not that he thought I was underqualified, rather, in his mind, the other role would be less demanding and, from his vantage point, was a better fit for someone my age.

His advice was not received as malicious. At that time, I believed he meant well. Admittedly, he was someone I'd grown to admire, so I was a little conflicted about the decision to apply. It took a lot of confidence to move forward with my decision and apply for the role—I had to dig deep. I reassured myself that I was not only fit for the job but was also capable of doing it.

When the co-founder got wind of the fact that I had applied for the position, he immediately called me to ask why I did not apply for the role he had recommended. I remember that Sunday morning as if it was yesterday; he spent two hours on the phone with me, trying to convince me to remove my name from the pool of candidates.

I felt intimidated. I was deflated for a while and even contemplated backing out. A good friend of mine told me that I should never allow anyone else to make decisions about my career trajectory and that if I want to back out, it should only be based on my own conviction.

As I reflected on the position I found myself in, to move forward with the process after the conversation with the co-founder, it could have easily been viewed as defiance. However, the advice from my other friend was just the nudge I needed to stay in the game.

I stuck with my initial decision to apply and went against what had now become the demands of my boss. On the day of the interview, to my surprise, he read the transcript of our conversation to the committee and shared with the team the things I had said in our private conversation, which were proof of why they should not consider me for the position and that I should instead apply for another position.

For a moment, I felt like waving the white flag in the face of an attempt to derail my decision to move forward. When I thought about it, although it would have been my way of surrendering to the opinion of someone who knew very little about me. I had to muster up the courage and remind myself that I was as fit as any other candidate for this position or opportunity.

I went through with the interview and was offered the position. Within months of my appointment to the role, who do you think was giving me great feedback about how well I was performing? You guessed it! The same person who discouraged me from applying for the job admitted that he was wrong about me. He misjudged my abilities.

We worked collaboratively on numerous grants and other fundraising ventures that yielded much success for the organization. Before long, he was singing my praises to others, and when it was time for me to move on, he expressed how much of a loss the institution would have suffered because of my departure.

How many times have you seen talented people have their flames extinguished by the limitations, wrongful judgments, and poor advice of others?

Conversely, I am sure we have also seen people who appear to be average doing extraordinary things because they have a stubborn allegiance to their purpose, more so than their critics. Even with the right intentions, we run the risk of giving others the power to prevent us from walking in our purpose and calling.

Confidence is like a staccato phrase that keeps replaying over and over in our minds, "I can do this." So, even if it doesn't come naturally for you, you should invest the time and energy to make it a priority on your personal development journey.

General and Specific Self Confidence

In an article published by Joan Marques and Satinder Dhiman, eds., Springer (2017), general self-confidence and specific self-confidence were highlighted[xliii].

The writers described general self-confidence as the belief in yourself to be successful regardless of the situations, tasks, experience, or expectations. Developing this image of self has a lot to do with your upbringing and the early influences and environments that you experienced during your formative years.

Growing up, were you affirmed and encouraged as a child? Were you told that you are better than your mistakes and that your failures were just a part of the journey? The affirmation or rebuke you received could profoundly impact the level of trust you have in yourself, ultimately resulting in greater or lower levels of self-confidence.

Chauna and I, at one point, became concerned about our oldest daughter Je'Chaun because we noticed she wasn't doing as well in school as we had expected. We did everything we could, with little to no success.

It was not until she was a little older that she told us about the verbal abuse she had endured in her kindergarten readiness program and how it had impacted her personality. I was devastated to know that my daughter had to go through such an experience. As parents, we wanted to help our child to regain her self-confidence. Although it took us a while—we did not give up but stayed committed.

One of the ways we did this was by affirming her on a consistent basis. We constantly reminded her how smart she was and that we believed in her. That she is worthy of the ground she stands on and deserves to occupy any space in which she finds herself. While this took some time, we believe that this was one of the best things we ever did for our child.

Specific Self Confidence

Having faith in our ability to complete a given task successfully at a particular time is referred to as specific self-confidence. According to the article, this confidence comes about due to the praise or affirmations that a person receives for their strong performance. With practice and effort one can achieve specific self-confidence.

Both general and specific self-confidence significantly impact the level at which we perform or influence others. Do you believe in your strengths and your capabilities? Do you, then accept and endorse them? Do you have enough trust in yourself and the things you can do, and to what extent can you influence others if given a chance?

General self-confidence comes through nurturing, while specific self-confidence comes through our giftedness (natural or cultivated) that others recognize and affirm. One can yield the latter through preparation and practice, eventually leading to perfection.

Regardless of whether you were fortunate to grow up in a nurturing environment, had some incredible inborn abilities, or had to learn and develop specific skills until you could master them, the bottom-line is that confidence is within our reach.

Before starting high school, I was a very confident kid.

I was aware of my intelligence because everybody in my small community reminded me of it at every turn. It was not uncommon for people in my community to stop me on the street, to offer words of affirmation, and let me know that they had very high expectations of me.

My peers would look to me for advice, and their parents would be happy whenever they were hanging out at my house. I would be given leadership roles in my small church, even when I thought I was not fully equipped to manage. My community invested in me.

Everything changed when I started high school. Based on my Common Entrance Exam scores, I was placed in the top high school in my parish. While there, some of my physical features, such as my gap tooth, lisp, and height, became the center of attention for my new schoolmates, and it was by no means a good thing. At home, my gap tooth reminded people that I was Timmy's son; at school, it was something I got bullied for.

My second week in school was a nightmare. My lisp was no longer cute, it was now a speech impediment. My thick Jamaican dialect was enough to make matters worse, even though I came from the rural side of town and had a relatively great mastery of the English Language. My classmates had nicknamed me "the patois king." I was facing in its truest sense—a real identity crisis.

My self-confidence went from a hundred to zero. I told my mother that I wanted to be transferred to another high school closer to home. My parents were not getting it, as far as they were concerned, I was in one of the best high schools in the country and assumed that things would get better eventually.

As the weeks progressed, the situation worsened. My confidence was in the trash, and I had no friends to lean on. I felt as if I was a 'nobody', and for the first time, I had lost all belief in my abilities. I considered myself inferior to everyone else in my classroom.

My favorite part of school was dismissal. I hated everything about school. I lied about having a headache to the teachers so I wouldn't have to answer any questions or speak openly. Obviously, I was dodging the possibility of being laughed at because of my impediments.

The semester finally ended, and my father came to my high school to meet with my teachers and collect my report card. I had nightmares in the days leading up to that moment. I knew it was going to be a disaster.

I was worried about the way my parents would feel about my extremely poor performance. If nothing else would convince them, I was certain that my poor performance would force them into considering my suggestion of a transfer from Saint Mary High School to Tacky High School.

I remember sitting through each meeting with my father as he listened to my teachers share the same line, "Jaymie has a lot of potential, but ..." My religious education teacher, Miss Frazer and my literature teacher, were the only teachers who told my father that I was brilliant and had a bright future ahead of me.

To put it mildly, my report card was horrible. I did not see myself bouncing back from this experience. As far as I was concerned, this was the end of my academic career. To make a bad situation even worse, knowing how hard my parents had worked in order to find the means to send me to that school, did not make this situation any easier. As the third child, I felt the full weight of expectations placed on me, and I'd let everyone down. There is more to come in this story—stay with me.

Impact of Low Self-Confidence

Based on The *Miriam-Webster Dictionary*, one acceptable definition of confidence is: "a feeling or consciousness of one's powers or of reliance on one's circumstances". It is believing in your ability to do well, regardless of how others may feel about it.[xliv]

There are a few things that will inevitably lead to low self-confidence. Depending on the frequency and degree to which you are exposed to these toxic elements they will have a negative effect on our confidence level. When your environment places little value on you as a person, if there is a lack of affirmation, and validation for what you bring to the table and if you are only reminded of your flaws, your level of confidence will diminish over time.

When you work in an environment where you are berated or face significant levels of denigration, it will weigh you down. Without some amount of self-belief to re-write the narrative in your mind, your critic's story will become the loudest voice. Eventually you will start believing it. This narrative is not the truth about you. In such cases, my advice is that you change the environment or start finding ways to neutralize that narrative either through self-regulation or if the situation allows, confronting it head on.

Many people fail to understand that a lack of self-confidence is a self-inflicted wound against their God-given abilities. Lack of self-confidence leads to what I call the Dangerous Five (5):

1. Insecurity
2. Mediocrity
3. Lack of trustworthiness
4. Reduced influence
5. Failure to maximize one's potential

Insecurity

In *"Leadership Gap: What Gets Between you and your Greatness,"* Lolly Daskal talks about ten signs that may show that you are an insecure leader or a leader who is low on confidence.[xlv]

She mentions that insecure leaders find it difficult to own their mistakes and tend to become defensive if they are being called out or challenged on their ideas, position, or the approach they are taking regarding a task or a project.

Insecurity in leaders make matters worse by preventing them from recognizing the worth of others on their team. They are locked into their own way of doing things, and the only feedback they are open to is a positive one.

Additionally, when experiencing this level of insecurity, these individuals will never admit when their decision yielded bad results and will be quick to cast blame in order to maintain their authoritative position.

In his book on Conversational Capacity, Craig Weber brilliantly explains how a person can inject life and energy into their team by maintaining a healthy balance between candor and curiosity[xlvi]. They can create a space and environment where their team can openly share opinions and perspectives and believe that their opinions will be regarded.

When a confident leader is challenged on an idea, his response would be "tell me more," instead of cutting the person off mid-sentence or criticizing those who disagree with him.

Team members find it hard to trust mentors who exhibit low self-confidence. The question that arises is, why should someone invest confidence in you if you are not able to invest confidence in your own abilities?

If you don't believe in a product yourself, it would be challenging to convince someone to buy it. There is always a need for leaders who inspire and motivate others to do more than their natural abilities allow them to achieve.

When a leader walks into a room, confident of their abilities, plans, and ideas, and a stubborn belief in their ability to inspire, their team members will overcome whatever challenges they will face in pursuit of excellence.

Confidence is contagious. Soon, others will catch on, and before long, your team will become unstoppable.

Insecure leaders lack the ability to persuade others. Imagine a member of the discalced community as a shoe salesman. Would you trust anything he says about the benefits of wearing shoes? I am sure you would send him on his way because he would have difficulty conveying with sincerity that the shoes in question are good for you.

Many leaders and their teams fail to expand because they fail to sell the vision and expectations with confidence and conviction. People must first believe that you believe in who you are before they buy into your idea.

Confidence allows you to celebrate your abilities and confront your weaknesses; confidently seek assistance through coaching, counseling, or mentorship to limit the impact of your weaknesses.

Low confidence forces leaders into a space of ease where they encounter minute challenges and minimal growth. Such leaders will only take on challenges when little is expected.

The natural progression of shying away from difficulties is mediocre results. What we must realize is that when faced with an impossible situation, your self-confidence and not your abilities will lead you towards achieving superior results. There are people who possess the ability, but because they lack the self-belief, they fail even to try.

How to Nurture and Develop Self-Confidence

We are the sum of our life experiences. Our exposure to positive parenting and a nurturing environment (to include our schools, churches, and the broader community) are factors that will have a profound impact on how confident we are as adults.

Scientists have now identified a direct correlation between a mother's pregnancy experience with the level of confidence their children will exhibit when they grow up.

It means that we will naturally display confident behaviors for factors beyond our control, or we may have to take steps through personal development to become more self-confident. In the next section, we will explore how we can successfully overcome the lack of confidence that impacts our ability to influence others positively.

Earlier in this chapter, I spoke about my early high school experience and how it shattered my confidence. I shared how horrible my report card was and that I felt as if my academic journey was closer to an end. The thing I remembered most after receiving my report card was the reaction of my father.

Although he had the absolute right, my father did not chastise me in the way I saw other parents doing to their children. He placed the report card in his back pocket, took me to a restaurant, and ordered us a delectable meal. After receiving our meals, he said to me, "Son, what I saw on that report card is not a reflection of the Jaymie I know." (I paraphrased my dialect a bit, but this statement captures the essence of what he had said).

The lumps in my throat were a clear indication that his words had pierced my soul. Looking back, I do not believe a flogging or just him yelling at me would have had the transformative effect that this statement did. His words were not just a reprimand. They offered me hope that even though I had messed up, I wasn't a mess.

When I got home later that evening, I went straight to bed, and my mother came and lay beside me. She also reassured me that we were going to bounce back from this. Her words furthered my self-esteem.

After that day, I dug my heels in, and I went to work. I studied hard, and I ignored the noise. At the end of that school year, I was placed third overall in that class behind two brilliant young ladies. My confidence was back, and I was ready to work.

We all have unique abilities and experiences. Also, a negative upbringing may rob us of the will to believe in who we are. I can guarantee that if you engage in the following methods, you can raise your self-esteem to a level that destructive criticism will be reduced to mere background noises in your journey to success.

1. Celebrate your strengths
2. Develop your own abilities
3. Secure mentorship
4. Be willing to accept feedback
5. Identify your weaknesses
6. Stretch yourself beyond your comfort zone

Celebrating your strengths is fundamental to building self-confidence. When we are fully aware of what we can do, it results in elevated levels of self-confidence and serves as the fuel to lead you into unchartered territory and come out victorious. Mike Tyson made a statement that I find intriguing. "Confidence breeds success, and success breeds confidence. Confidence applied properly will surpass genius."[xlvii] It rightly implies that success is sure to follow when anything starts with confidence, and natural cycles of success will ensue beyond that.

Often, we tend to focus on our weaknesses, especially when faced with a new task or assignment. We allow self-doubt to have the advantage as we spend most of our time mulling over questions such as, "Am I smart enough to do this?", "What if I fail?" or "Am I making a total fool of myself?". When you know you have a handle on your strengths, you already know the answers to these questions.

Here is how to counter the questions with roots firmly planted in self-doubt: "I can do this...even if I fail or mess up, I am capable, and will eventually figure it out".

Katty Kay and Claire Shipman wrote an incredible book called *The Confidence Code*, an excellent resource I would recommend for (particularly for female) leaders seeking to build self-confidence[xlviii]. What struck me in this body of work is the way they relate self-confidence to achievement. The essence of their work is that our confidence grows as we continue to succeed. What better way to do this than to focus on our strengths?

I've witnessed my colleagues who missed out on

promotions because they chose not to apply for a position under the assumption that they were not sure if they could do the job. Usually, their reason for not throwing their hats in the ring is that they were too focused on their gaps and weaknesses while ignoring their strengths.

I recall one of my friends sharing with me his apprehension about applying for a position that his manager had recommended to him. His fear was that even though he was doing well now, receiving a lot of great reviews from his customers and colleagues, the standard of performance would be much higher in this role, and he didn't feel that he could measure up.

At that time, I was investing more belief in his abilities than he was. He had a knack for relationship-building. It was something that I perceived as one of his greatest strengths. I was also aware that in a leadership role, it was a trait that would serve him very well.

I helped him focus on leveraging his strengths as part of the narrative he would use along his leadership journey. Since that time, he has landed several promotions and has become a sought-after prospect on LinkedIn for multiple other job offers in Fortune 500 companies.

You don't have to be good at everything to win at something. Instead, you must first acknowledge and then celebrate the things that you are good at. In this regard, the statement by John Maxwell rings true: "We spend too much time repairing and not enough time preparing." It is always best to lead with your strengths.

After you have identified your strengths, the next step is to surround yourself with experts, such as mentors and coaches, who can help you leverage your strengths and limit your blind spots. Through mentors, we have an unprecedented opportunity to benefit from the attainments of those who have blazed the path before us.

Further, when we fail to invest in our personal development, it increases the likelihood of us becoming envious when others do. We begin to see the results that it yields for them.

One of the things I am keen to observe as I watch the NBA is the noticeable differences between players who invest in developing themselves instead of those who merely rely on their innate abilities.

The scoreboard bears a record of the sizeable difference in their stats. Kobe Bryant was famous for hiring coaches to help with the specific areas in which he needed to grow. As leaders, we should never take for granted that we are naturally endowed with certain traits. We should always be willing to invest in our overall development.

Regardless of how talented you are as a leader, coach, parent, educator, athlete, or artist, everyone can benefit from mentorship. Someone who has already walked the path and has already made the mistakes can offer valuable support in navigating the hurdles or roadblocks we may face.

It is also important for me to highlight that a mentor does not have to meet a specific age requirement. I've heard senior executives refer to individuals who were far younger than they were as mentors. These individuals have spent a lot of time honing a specific craft and now have a wealth of knowledge and expertise that can enhance your journey.

Mentors can also help you to see your blind spots. The affirmation and feedback provided through mentorship will inspire your confidence and lead to better decision-making. Mentorship also inspires resilience. You have a trusted guide who will help you resiliently bounce back after each failure.

In addition to mentorship and personal development, we should also be willing to accept feedback. Feedback is vital to identifying the areas where improvement could make a difference.

Positive feedback helps us realize whether our approach is right and affirms our strengths, whereas negative feedback tells us something is going wrong. In both cases, we can mine a wealth of information that can help us continue to do great things for which we receive affirmation and stop doing those things which impair our progress.

It is important to understand that negative feedback does not amount to discouragement. Thus, we need not lose our self-confidence because of negative feedback but instead perceive it as constructive criticism. It is also important to filter this feedback through the prism of qualified expert opinion or personal intuition. Preference should be given to expert opinions more so than personal feelings when evaluating the feedback we receive.

Your confidence increases when you have your blind spots covered. All Quarterbacks have blind spots or vulnerable areas, but their coaches place defensive players in certain positions to protect them. When quarterbacks know that their blind spots are covered, they can focus on their strength, passing the ball to their teammates for a touchdown.

Finally, growing in confidence requires that you stretch yourself beyond your comfort zone. Why is this important? Too often, people lose relevance because they remain in the same position of ease and comfort out of their fear of failure.

It would be meaningless to dedicate another chunk of the book to this topic, as we have already analyzed failure thoroughly in an early chapter. However, it is important and relevant to mention that our confidence grows as we conquer and we engage in stretching. Stretching beyond our comfort zone will always bring about some amount of discomfort. However, at times, it is required for you to precisely discover the hidden talents and uncover unknown opportunities.

Confidence in Action

Even if you are not a confident person naturally, there are some basic behaviors that you should know about and practice to exude strong self-confidence.

Barbara Patcher, the author of the book: *Essentials of Business Etiquette*, said, "I believe that if you project a confident, credible, composed image, people will respond to you as if you are all those things. Who cares what you are feeling on the inside?"[xlix]

Barbara's point of view aligns very closely with the perspective of some of the experts that I have mentioned earlier in the book. One of the hallmarks of a confident leader is tied to their ability to secure the admiration of their team and organization by carefully managing the way they speak, dress, and present through their body language, both during one-on-one and team interactions. Your self-confidence seeps out in these behaviors. It is also an opportunity for you to shape the image of you, that your team will hold onto as they look to you for leadership.

Body Language

Our non-verbal communication is a very powerful part of the way we communicate and project confidence. In an article entitled *Nonverbal Communication and Body Language*, Segal Et al. proffered: "When your nonverbal signals match up with the words you're saying, they increase trust, clarity, and rapport. When they don't, they can generate tension, mistrust, and confusion."[l]

You give off non-verbal cues in your facial expressions, posture while sitting, standing, and even the way you walk. Being aware of the appropriate posture in a particular setting may feel a little overwhelming. However, I strongly suggest that you educate yourself on the things that make you come off as less confident and avoid such behaviors.

There is a wealth of information on this subject that could inform you of this aspect of your professional development. Although most of the advice given is gender specific, I urge you to dig deeper into this, nonetheless.

Nick Morgan also suggests in his book *Power Cues* that, "Our body language plays a critical role in the level of confidence we project." Here are a few of the suggestions he made[li]:

1. Standing up straight with your shoulders back helps you come across as confident and commanding, while slouching and looking down at your feet have the opposite effect.

2. When seated, resist the urge to slouch, as this makes you appear as a subordinate and not authoritative enough.

3. To come across as open and friendly with someone you hardly know, you should keep your hands uncrossed and preferably by your side. Your torso should be pointed towards the person and remain open.

Facial expressions are also a dead giveaway of what is going on in our minds. A smile, a frown, or even a smirk are indicators of how you truly feel on the inside. People can also use our facial expressions to gauge our confidence levels.

Are you making eye contact when someone is speaking? Are you coming off as nervous as that uncomfortable smile on your face shows? People can know if your smile is genuine by whether your smile reaches your eyes. I am not claiming to be an expert on facial expressions; however, in my coaching sessions, I consider it important enough to encourage my clients to be aware of this important aspect of their deportment.

Speech

When it comes to our speech, our tone of voice, our diction, our energy, and even our grasp of grammar are all important factors that people will use to gauge our level of confidence. People can decide whether you are smart and capable by analyzing the way you express yourself in meetings and presentations. If they can't hear or understand what you are saying, you leave them with little or no reason to invest any confidence in what you are claiming.

Whenever I am getting ready to speak, I go over my presentation or speech a minimum of three times to make sure that I am 100% prepared. Whenever I don't do this, it affects the quality of my delivery in a negative way. The key here is preparation and effort. The more prepared you are to speak, it heightens your level of confidence when it is time to deliver.

It is true that people are drawn to you on the basis of your appearance and posture, but your words, coupled with the energy in your delivery, provide them with an insight into your mind space. Through the power of speech, you can shape the perception that others have of you. I urge you not to neglect the power inherent in speech.

One important question to consider before you speak

is: "how will my message be received?"

There are some people who have a very high level of discernment in detecting when you are just trying to fill the air with words. In such instances - might I pause here and suggest Plato's words? "The wise speaks because he has something to say, a fool speaks because he has to say something." - do not speak only because you want to come off as brilliant. You should consider the relevance and usefulness of what you are saying to the discussions on hand.

I know you have heard people say things like, I was floored by our conversation, and I would listen to him or her all day. People gather a great deal from conversations, and every conversation or speech gives you a new opportunity to create a positive impact, adding value to the lives of others using the power of words.

Dress

There is an expression that we casually use, but I consider it to be very profound in conveying the significance of our appearance. The expression goes, "Dress to Impress." We run the risk of losing people when we neglect this vital aspect of our appearance. To ignore the power of the eyes is a big mistake by leaders.

Let's face it, that is how the human mind works. Securing some amount of credibility even before being given the opportunity to speak a word is not an opportunity we should take lightly.

Carmine Gallo agrees with this, as she opined, "We size people up as soon as they walk into a room. The first thing we often do is—like it or not – notice a person's clothes"[lii]. If fashion is not your strong suit (pun not intended), you can always secure the help of experts (personal shoppers, fashion consultants, or fashion blogs) to help you with this. Just be aware that your style to dress is an essential aspect of your personality.

Benefits of Confidence

Confidence allows you to show up, forge forward and compete, regardless of competition, challenges, and criticism. When you are a confident leader, you will:

1. Secure trust
2. Nurture ambition
3. Motivate and inspire others
4. Take calculated risks

It is easier to trust confident people, and numerous studies support this fact. Galinsky and Kilduff produced research data that demonstrated, "The snap judgment people make when they witness confidence in action will cause them to regard those who display confident behaviors higher than those who don't."[liii]

For example, suppose there is a room full of senior-level executives listening to a presentation by two sales representatives, where one comes off as confident. At the same time, the other one is informative but less confident. In that case, it is highly probable that the confident one will close the deal.

Before they believe in you, people want to see whether you believe in yourself. With confidence, you can win their trust, and when people trust you, they find it easier to buy into what you are selling, whether it is an idea, solution, or a vision. We all know that trust is a fundamental variable in securing results, forging relationships, and leading, for that matter.

One of the most remarkable scenes in the movie, *The Pursuit of Happyness*, is when Will Smith finally lands an interview for his dream job on Wall Street, after experiencing numerous setbacks and challenges, dealing with family problems, homelessness, and joblessness.

He showed up late on the morning of his interview, after a series of unfortunate occurrences, resulting in him being inappropriately attired. When asked a rhetorical question about hiring someone who shows up late to an interview and without a shirt, Will Smith retorts, "He must have been wearing some really great pants."

His response was not only confidently expressed, but it also eases the tension in a situation that could have been very heavy. With his confidence and humor, he disarms his prospective boss and landed the dream job. Confidence has a way of breaking down barriers, leading others to trust you and invest in your idea.

Confidence allows a leader to be ambitious in his mindset, planning, and execution. Ambitious leaders make bold and courageous decisions. Many people fail to win big because they lead from a place of fear and a lack of confidence. They see things for the challenges they come with. On the contrary, confident leaders see the challenges, but their focus lies on opportunities.

Confidence gives you the determination to exceed expectations and go beyond your comfort zone to establish new limits. There are individuals who view ambition in a negative light — elevating humility as a more effective and admirable trait. Ambition and humility are not mutually exclusive principles. One can be humble and ambitious at the same time.

Had it not been for ambitious people, we would not be able to celebrate the numerous breakthroughs we are experiencing today as a civilized nation. Confidence inspires ambition. A confident person makes it challenging for society to maintain the status quo.

I remember a meeting where we were discussing a longstanding issue, for which an important decision needed to be made. Each time, the leaders voted against the proposed solutions. After that meeting, I expressed my frustration at the indecisiveness of my colleagues with one of my mentors.

My mentor responded with a statement that I will never forget. He said, "Many people want a turkey as the centerpiece on the Thanksgiving table, but rarely does anyone want to wring the neck of the turkey." As gross as that sounded to me as a vegetarian, I could see sense in that statement. Confident and ambitious people don't find it excruciating to make decisions. Confident leaders naturally inspire and motivate their teams and network to think, grow, and execute.

I recall sitting in my first planning meeting as a Vice Principal with my boss and listening to her as she shared her vision for the school and the role corresponding role she wanted everyone to play in achieving these goals and objectives.

She was clear on what she wanted. She was convinced that her ideas would work, she was willing to go the extra mile, even if no one else was willing to accompany her along the journey. She firmly expressed belief in her skills and vision to bring change.

I was motivated and inspired by her confidence. I was sold at that moment, and I was ready to go the extra mile to align my efforts with her goals and vision. It was the beginning of a remarkable tenure with a confident and dynamic leader who drove our team towards successfully materializing these goals.

As I close this chapter I will borrow a few words from my friend and mentor in leadership Dr. Glen Baker. Confidence is by far one of the most essential traits of effective leaders. To be an effective leader, one must be able to motivate, inspire and influence others. This will not happen with a timid and tentative leader. An effective leader must believe in themselves and be confident in their own judgment and decision-making ability. Confidence also empowers a leader to not be afraid to take risks or to set and strive for goals that might seem impossible. One must believe in themselves if they are going to be a true leader.

Reflection Questions: Confidence

- How has your childhood experiences shaped the level of confidence you currently exude as a leader?

- Describe one occasion in which confidence or the lack of it affected you within the professional setting?

- Which of the following areas do you struggle with the most and how will you improve on this moving forward:

  - Facial Expressions and Body Language
  - Dress
  - Speech

Chapter Eight:
Energy

"Energy, not time, is the fundamental currency of high performance." – Tony Schwartz

What is that one factor that fuels curiosity, inspires a culture of high performance, and inspires meaningful and considerable change? You guessed it! It's energy. When a leaders steps into a space, they bring something to that space that profoundly impacts culture and behavior.

Energy is the most critical currency of a successful leader. The job of a leader is to motivate and inspire their team to unlock hidden strengths, shatter glass ceilings and lead with transformation. It is impossible for a leader to achieve this without harnessing and exuding the right energy.

Whether casting a vision, speaking life into teammates, or navigating an impossible crisis, a leader should never underestimate the inherent success that can emanate from leveraging the transformational power of energy.

Energy is attractive in humans! It is our attraction to it that fills up seats at national conferences. The promise of a stimulating, thought-provoking, and enlightening experience is so alluring; it captivates our attention and satisfies our curiosity.

I have witnessed energy in leadership firsthand. I have seen the transformative effect of energy as a superpower in driving change and success, while building a high-performance culture. Delmas Campbell and Nicole Hughes were both principals I looked up to as leaders of the historic Pine Forge Academy. While their leadership styles were different, they both brought an immeasurable amount of positive energy to their roles.

They knew exactly how to ignite passion within the team through their words and demeanor. Whenever they entered a room, the atmosphere changed. They had a compelling way of selling a vision that almost always compelled action on the part of their audience.

By its definition, energy is the strength and vitality required for sustained mental and physical activities. If we were to redefine energy within the context of leadership, we would conclude that energy is a primary component that drives a leader to build a strong and effective organizational culture by motivating others to remain optimistic, innovative, and committed to the overall vision.

In the dullest of circumstances, when energy is applied, it has an electrifying effect on everyone within its sphere. To develop the ability to inspire and energize others, we must systematically generate and nurture the right kind of energy.

Brendon Burchard tells leaders to "bring joy," and I believe this is truly one of the most crucial roles of a leader. Inspired by your leadership skills, people should find the drive and motivation to keep going in the face of difficulties.

Leadership without energy is like an automobile without an engine. Energy in leadership adds life to a dull room; it excites others who were otherwise dormant. It moves people from a state of apathy to a place of hope and belief.

Positive and Negative Energy

In the movie *The Proposal*, Sandra Bullock played the role of Margaret Tate, a very confident and poised chief editor who from all indications, could also be labeled a megalomaniac. In her first appearance with her team, we see a shining example of the type of energy a leader should never bring to a room.

As she stepped off the elevator and enters the floor, we saw a dramatic shift in the atmosphere. Team members rushed to their keyboards to alert others of her presence. The room, which was full of life, happiness, and enthusiasm, immediately plunged into a place where people desperately scampered to their desks, doing everything they could to be invisible.

Whether positive or negative, we all bring some energy with us as we enter a room. Leaders who want to inspire transformation, growth and solid results must be cognizant of the type of energy they exude. Energy is magnetic when it is positive and uplifting, but repulsive and toxic when it is negative.

Some people have the uncanny ability to absorb all the positive energy from a room or discussion. Whenever they speak in meetings, the room is always silenced. No one is interested in offering an alternate opinion, fearing that their ideas will be extinguished. I have personally witnessed this. If you were there, you could feel the life and positive energy evaporate at that moment.

Bruce Schneider is one of the foremost authorities on this subject. His body of work highlights two distinct types of energy: catabolic and anabolic energy[liv]. Catabolic and Anabolic energy represent both ends of the spectrum. When encumbered with difficulties, pressure, or stress, individuals are apt to display catabolic energy. This is often manifested in the defensiveness of the person; they struggle to accept feedback or surrender to the opposing argument with no meaningful input or counterargument in a passive-aggressive way.

We all have difficult moments or, in some cases, long-term situations that will negatively affect our emotional state. If this remains unchecked, it can ultimately affect the kind of energy we display. This type of energy leaves employees feeling scapegoated and anxious because leaders tend to pass blame and inspires unhealthy conflict (Schneider).

It is highly unlikely that a leader would intentionally allow their negative energy to serve as an impediment to the success of their team and organization. Therefore, when we discern negativity in our energy, we are in a much better position to manage it. The last thing we want is to be the source of dysfunctionality and toxicity in our team because of our failure to gauge and effectively manage our catabolic energy.

When a leader mostly engages anabolic energy, their likelihood of success is increased. This is evidenced by our celebrating and embracing the contribution of others (Schneider). When we welcome suggestions and ideas from others, allowing those around us to feel valued and heard we are building a high-performance culture. This form of energy allows us to embrace the benefit of differences and not allow prejudices and biases to hold us as prisoners.

Every leader's goal or dream is to see their entire team saturated with anabolic energy—having the drive to build strong teams, serve each other, view every situation with a fresh set of eyes, and find meaning and importance in every potential solution with a willingness to question their position.

Impact of Low Energy

If your mood or energy is off, people can sense it from the moment you walk through the door. People depend on you to inject life into their day.

Each team member experiences their own cycles of productivity and sluggishness, and given how contagious energy can be, they will feed off the energy you are bringing. Just as streams need current to move, people need your energy to move. Your energy level, as a leader, is also linked to the level of productivity of your team.

Reflect on a time when you worked with someone who displayed high levels of catabolic energy. What was it like for you? Did you have an enjoyable experience? Did you feel motivated or inspired to show up in the mornings and produce your best work? I am certain that this kind of workplace would not rank very highly on your list of *Best Places to Work*.

When we operate consistently from a place of negative energy, we have difficulties getting things done. Think about a time in your life when you found yourself in this situation. Personally, reduced energy has a profoundly negative impact on my level of productivity. When I am low on energy, I find it difficult to motivate, inspire, and drive change in others.

How can you motivate others if you are not motivated? When your energy level or motivation is depleted, this has a ripple effect on your performance because your team depends on you. The key role for leaders is to **inspire and motivate** their teams to perform at their highest level, and there is no way you can do this while running on "E."

You often have team members performing below their potential because they are not challenged or encouraged to commit to going the extra mile. Leaders with low or negative energy will struggle to get the best out of their team.

These leaders find it challenging to gain buy-in with their vision or idea because they lack this high-energy disposition. Excitement, charisma, and eccentricity is beyond their natural abilities. What do you do in this case? Do you surrender to the forces of nature and allow your team's success to be negatively impacted by this?

"Leadership is influence...nothing more, nothing less"—(Maxwell)[lv]. You do not always have to be an upbeat person to influence your team. There are some people who are drawn to the enigmatic characteristics of a leader, who may not have high energy but are clearly committed to their own vision. This passion comes through regardless of natural disposition.

You do not have to be a slick, fast-talking leader to energize your team. Energy is about inspiring people to see who they are and where they need to be; allowing them to feel like they have the ability within them to achieve their goals. When this happens, few things remain impossible for this leader and team.

The Seven Levels of Energy

Schneider's body of work essentially proffers that the sum of our experiences, values, and assumptions is either limited or expanded as we use these filters to interpret what we see. He proposes that there are seven levels of energy displayed by leaders. Table 2.0 provides a brief description of each of these levels:

Table 2.0

Ego Level	Energy Level	Core Thoughts	Core Feelings	Actions and Behaviors
Strong Ego	One (1)	Victim	Apathy	Lethargy
	Two (2)	Conflict	Anger	Defiance
Low Ego	Three (3)	Responsibility	Forgiveness	Cooperation
	Four (4)	Concern	Compassion	Service
	Five (5)	Reconciliation	Peace	Acceptance
No Ego	Six (6)	Creative	Joy	Visionary
	Seven (7)	Non-judgement	Absolute Passion	Creation

Source: Bruce Schneider
(2006)—Energy Leadership

The idea here is that as a leader moves up each level of the energy spectrum, their influence grows. The goal is to move from level one to seven in each area of our lives. At the first (1st) level, the leader blames someone else for everything that happens to them. At the second (2nd) level, the leader moves from being a victim to becoming a bully. When cornered, they push back hard. Fear and intimidation are tactics that leaders at this level use to prompt action on the part of their teammates.

At the third (3rd) level, this leader's behavior becomes a little more mature, and they're more accepting and rational in their thinking. At level four (4), these leaders tend to be great team players. Their behavior now becomes way more collaborative, but they are also hungry for approval and recognition for their work. At level five (5), leaders tend to think about the big picture and can solve problems in an efficient way by transforming challenges into opportunities.

Leaders at level six (6) of Schneider's model attract opportunities wherever they go, so they are highly sought after. The seventh and final level of the model encompasses people willing to create opportunities for others to reside. They are not into winning for themselves at all, but rather, making room for others. They are also less judgmental of the actions and behaviors of others.

According to Schneider, the idea here is that no leader sits at just one level in every aspect of leadership. We vacillate between levels, but often, we spend a lot of time at one level, which dominates our respective styles. Our goal is to apply various strategies, the prime among them – awareness to be elevated to the level we need to be, based on our leadership goals.

Harnessing and Preserving Energy

There are many days when I feel like I want to be as far away as possible from the office or meetings. Given a choice, I would much rather be at the gym or on a soccer field playing in a league. Some may question my sanity after reading this. How can meetings or time in the office be more draining than running for 45 minutes on a treadmill?

We underestimate how draining the demands of work can be on our physical, emotional, intellectual, and spiritual energy. Meetings, strategic planning sessions, and resolving interpersonal conflicts will make a 90-minute soccer game feel like a walk in the park. If you don't have the fighting power to bring the right energy to these situations, you will struggle with burnout.

We are multi-dimensional beings—possessing physical, emotional, intellectual, and spiritual energy that we must manage separately to remain effective. "I don't have the mind space to tackle this subject today; my brain is fried. Can we take this on after the weekend?" These are some of the signals we send whenever our energy levels have waned. In this section, we will look at each of these dimensions and suggest ways in which we can effectively harness and preserve enough fighting power to sustain us on our journey.

Intellectual Energy

Intellectual Energy controls our ability to think and understand ideas and information. With all the struggles of daily life, our intellectual energy is an essential aspect of our functionality. In our consulting practice, we help our clients measure the cognitive abilities of prospective employees to ensure that when hired, their new employees can process information at an acceptable speed.

In a conversation with a senior executive in healthcare, she shared that when considering a new hire, she heavily weighs the learning curve of that person as part of the selection process. No one has the bandwidth to do another person's job for an extended period. For this reason, your cognitive abilities must be stimulated and preserved.

Our intellectual energy helps us process complex information with clarity to simplify decision-making and accelerate the learning process. Tony Schwartz and

Catherine McCarthy wrote an excellent piece addressing some of the ideas leaders should focus on to manage all energy levels effectively.[lvi]

One of the strategies they suggested to preserve our intellectual energy is tied to the way we manage distractions. The writers claimed that if we start focusing on one task at a time and minimize distractions, we will reduce the likelihood of intellectual exhaustion.

At work, our phones are ringing or pinging away with numerous notifications and reminders. Our computers chime, signaling the arrival of a new email, and the alert on our watches tells us it's time to go for a walk and stretch our legs. Each of these distractions is competing for our attention. Schwartz and McCarthy indicated that we are likely to take more time to complete a task because of these distractions.

Another suggestion the writers made was prioritizing challenging tasks to avoid the possibility of stressful situations later. The way we manage distractions and stressful assignments can deplete our intellectual energy. We should ensure that our approach is helping us to use our energy in the most efficient way possible.

Emotional Energy

Our ability to recognize our own feelings and the feelings of others is fueled by our emotional energy. Our **Emotional Energy** allows us to read the room and connect with our team in a meaningful way. On a personal level, this energy enables you to drive exceptional results because your team members know that you are relatable.

You connect with their needs with a willingness to address their challenges while creating opportunities.

Craig Groeschel said, "You cannot lead at the highest level of love from the deepest part of your heart when you are emotionally empty."[lvii] At its peak, emotional energy allows you to secure discretionary value from your team as you tackle projects requiring intense psychological commitment. The easiest way to harness and sustain emotional energy is awareness and recovery.

When we fail to listen to our emotional cues and plan for our own emotional recovery, we end up exerting more catabolic, rather than anabolic, energy. It happens when our anxiety or fight and flight responses are activated and often send us down a path of negative emotions that may cause our judgment to be clouded. When we operate on fight or flight mode, we are unable to think clearly, logically, and reflectively (Schwartz and McCarthy).

Physical Energy

Our physical energy is by far the most consequential of all our energies. Our body is the home of our emotional, intellectual, and spiritual faculties. It carries us wherever we go. We must invest time and intentionality in the way we treat our bodies. Physical energy depletes when we fail to follow proper health principles related to nutrition, exercise, and rest.

Here are a few tips you can practice to harness and preserve your physical energy:

1. Rest: There is no substitute for good rest. When we allow our bodies to rest, we experience the

three "Rs": relaxation, recovery, and repair. Experts recommend six to eight hours of sleep each day for our body and brain cells to fully recover and for damaged cells to repair in our bodies.

2. Nutrition: Time at work can take away from our ability to eat nutritionally balanced meals. Should we fail to practice healthy eating, we run the risk of other problems emerging, such as life-threatening illnesses, obesity, fatigue, and eating disorders.

3. Exercise: Working out three times per week for a minimum of 45 minutes is recommended for those who want to remain physically agile. Taking walk breaks throughout the day has also proven to be a great way to reinvigorate.

When you invest in your health, you automatically experience higher productivity levels in all other aspects of your life. In the same way that athletes must balance their rest, nutrition, and diet to remain at the top of their game, we also have a duty to stay at our best. Spare no expense to take care of your physical health. Pay for that gym membership, hire that trainer, buy the right kind of food, take that long-awaited trip to the spa; do what you must to preserve your physical energy. Trust me when I say this: your body will thank you.

Spiritual Energy

Our spiritual energy is what gives us our sense of purpose. As a man of faith, I prioritize this aspect of who I am more than any other aspect of my life. My purpose or reason for being is at the core of every coaching session, business deal, speaking engagement, or workshop that I participate in. When applying this concept on a personal level, keep in mind that your spiritual energy is what drives you to create a lasting impact and indelible mark on those you serve. You will often hear people say things like, "I have totally lost my way," or "I am clueless. Why am I even here?"

A strong sense of purpose has a stabilizing effect in an ever-changing world. It regulates our morals, values, and behaviors. In the face of promotions, achievements, or even failure, it is great to have a system in place that keeps you anchored and stable.

So, my first word of advice in this regard is to decide—what is your reason for existence. What on earth are you here to do? Once you hone this idea, it should serve as the driving force and key motivational factor behind your behaviors and actions.

Energy Cycles

Understanding our energy cycle is a crucial aspect of our success journey. Our energy cycles dance in synchrony with the various timelines of our lives. I am a creationist, and the six-day creative cycle, followed by a rest day, is one way we can infer that while navigating the various energy cycles, the highs, and lows both play a role in our journey.

As human beings, we should deepen our awareness of our energy cycle, so we operate efficiently and optimally, based on what's required. Our energy cycles are made up of days, weeks, months, seasons, and even our life.

Our daily energy cycle is predicated on how we manage our time daily. Do we have a routine that helps us get our best work when it matters the most? For example, my day starts at 5:00 AM, and the first thing I do at the start of my day is to pray and meditate. Right after, I get my exercise in, as it helps to freshen up for the day.

There are two things that make it easier for me to do this. Firstly, I am well rested and have the energy to take on the rigor of exercise at this time of the morning. On the days I do work out early, I tend to have more energy throughout the day because my exercise helps me to release endorphins that give me a greater drive to achieve.

I usually schedule the most rigorous activities in my day for the mornings because, based on my daily energy cycle, I feel I have the bandwidth to make the best decisions and put in maximum effort. Depending on how aware we are of our energy cycle, we can shorten our usual 8–12-hour day into a 5-hour day, allowing us to dedicate more time to other things.

Not only will you need to understand your daily energy cycle, but you will also need to understand your monthly energy cycle. Some organizations have a natural rhythm in the way they operate—with standard monthly meetings and reports that are due at specific times. When you know this and seek to synchronize your energy cycle with these cycles, you are more likely to reduce the possibility of anxiety, burnout, and exhaustion.

I would like to expand this view of the energy cycle to specific seasons of our lives as well. As leaders, we go through different seasons of our lives and career, and if we manage our time and energy cycle well, we can maximize on the most crucial moments that form the foundation for a strong and successful tenure. For example, Pierre Quinn, in one of our interviews, stresses the importance of emerging leaders maximizing the learning opportunities present within the first 3-6 months of taking on a leadership role.

This suggestion is brilliant for many reasons, but I want to point out the most important ones. When you are newly appointed, the energy surrounding you is more likely to be positive. There will be people lining up to answer all the questions you have about the culture and practices of the organization.

Even though you are being evaluated from the moment you sit in the chair, you can also bank on the fact that you will be graded on a curve because you are new—this is a perfect time to ride the waves of naivety as well as the honeymoon phase by remaining curious and objective to ensure you get the very best out of that season. It will serve as the ideal foundation for a long and successful career.

Our lives in general also operate within various energy cycles. I tell my girls that they should develop healthy habits while they are young, as these habits will define who they become. From youth to old age, we go through cycles of energy. Depending on the decisions we make within these energy cycles, we can build a strong foundation to pave the path forward.

At the age of 35, most athletes are on the other side of the curve of their energy cycle. If they failed to break records or put in the hall of fame performance while they were supposed to be at their peak, they may risk injury to make up for this lost time.

Our bodies are strong and can handle the things we throw at them, but when we fail to identify signals indicating that it is time for a break, we become disruptors of our energy cycle, which can prove detrimental over the long haul. Sometimes, our body and mind have an excellent read of what is going on with us, and they present it by leaving us feeling depleted of energy.

We should never view the low aspects of our energy cycle as a bad thing but rather, receive it as a message to re-evaluate, regroup or just relax so that we can feel refueled and re-energized for the next energy cycle.

Understanding our daily, weekly, monthly, and seasonal energy cycles will help us become more efficient, productive, and successful. We can plan our routine to be most efficient when we have the most energy to produce the best work, and rest and relax when our energy runs low.

Benefits of Energy

Tony Robbins, a New York Times bestselling author,

philanthropist, and the nation's number one life and business strategist, says, "The higher your energy level, the more efficient your body. The more efficient your body, the better you feel and the more you will use your talent to produce outstanding results."[lviii] The bottom line is that it takes energy to get things done.

Leaders with high levels of anabolic energy:

1. Captivate the attention and focus of their team
2. Mobilize their teams to act
3. Drives change and momentum
4. Creates urgency

People like excitement; they like to be around people with a flare in their bones to get things done in a passionate way. This kind of energy drives a team to success. Team members are always looking for fuel to get going. A leader who has the energy and the willingness to motivate his team will experience greater levels of success; more so than other leaders with similar leadership gifts but display high levels of catabolic energy.

Having the technical knowledge or experience in each area is an important part of being an effective leader, but if you lack the energy to connect with people, your knowledge or experience will do very little to bring you the results you need.

High energy leadership is a must if you want to capture the attention of your audience, team, or clients. It automatically comes with a drive to accomplish and deliver results. High energy leaders always go after results. They are interested in getting their team excited about an idea or project. I call high energy leaders gap leaders in that High energy leaders take pleasure in stepping up and seeking out opportunities to keep the team engaged.

High energy leaders are like a quarterback on a football team or point guards on a basketball team. They like to be highly involved and are always ready to move the ball and take their team to higher heights. They set the tone for their team and, sometimes, for the entire organization.

Consequently, their high positive energy draws people towards them. These high-energy people are always looking for a meaning and reason to be engaged. They even look for a reason to come to work. Some people accept that they are not the life of the party or have no potential to bring the life, but they thrive when they are associated with high energy individuals.

Innovation and enthusiasm

Energy drives innovation and enthusiasm. It brings out the best in a team—they start viewing obstacles as challenges that can be defeated. People like to be in a working environment that is filled with fun, passion, and enthusiasm. This environment breeds innovation and growth. A team that is charged up and energized can surmount any challenge. Leaders have to activate the superpower that team members possess – the power to perform at their best, which also enables them to be innovative. That power is a hidden energy that must be tapped into for excellence.

It's interesting to watch professional teams and their coaches. There is always a player or a coach who drives the energy. There is always a team member who gives the team that magic factor that sets them ablaze when it seems as if they are about to be overtaken by defeat or fear. Energy adds extra legs to a person's will or drive to push forward in the face of opportunities or obstacles. It's like watching Draymond Green of the Golden State Warriors. He is never out of energy and is always pushing his team to tap into that hidden inner strength.

When I was in college, I remember working with a sales team selling books and magazines. I hated every minute of it, and my results were a testament to my displeasure with this job. I spent long hours in the sun each day, knocking on doors, desperately trying to sell books. The days were long, and the returns were discouraging. There were days when I came home having sold only one book. It was a rough experience.

The first leg of the summer work program was over, and I was allowed to go home and enjoy the rest of my summer—away from the fruitless sales job that I took on. Unlike other members of the team, I was not able to quit. I had worked for two months, and I was nowhere near my goal for the summer—I needed that money to get registered for the upcoming semester. I was depressed and totally out of it. I wanted to give up and quit, but it was too late, and I only had three weeks left to do what I had failed to do all summer.

With nowhere else to go, I decided to tap into my faith and try to do things a little differently. There were a few things that I did that I believe led to a 360 turnaround for me.

1. I spent at least an hour each night before bed reflecting and meditating on my core purpose/faith.
2. I exercised every night before going to bed and in the morning before heading out to work.
3. I invested in healthy meals.
4. I ensured I got eight hours of sleep each night.
5. I greeted my potential customers with a big smile and a firm handshake.
6. I walked with urgency and confidence.
7. I connected with someone who was high energy, and I modeled some of his daily practices.

At the end of the three weeks, I was not granted the award of 'best salesman', but I could make enough money to complete my registration for my final year in college. I jumped from making ten and twenty dollars a day to consistently making between a hundred and three hundred dollars a day. That was a significant transformation for me. That was when I discovered that if you deliberately invest in generating energy, you will experience growth and improved results.

Encourage energy

Leaders must make it a high priority to affirm team members who display high energy and passion. Leaders must compliment team members who display urgency when undertaking a given task or project. Building a high-energy culture can be scary for those who view high energy as challenging work or extra effort. Not all persons are wired automatically with high energy; that does not mean that they are without potential—there will always be things that send them screaming or yelling with excitement. Everybody has something that excites them; not everybody responds to excitement in an easily recognizable way.

It is the leader's responsibility to assist team members in finding their sweet spot so that they can use that high-level energy to achieve growth and success. It is not a bad thing to deliberately create a high-energy environment. A high-level, high-energy environment normally produces high-level results.

Some leaders are not equipped to use their energy in a positive way. This can cause even greater damage to a team's morale and growth—more than a leader with low energy. If the leader has negative energy, the entire team suffers and splinters. While the working environment needs energy, leaders must allow team members to use their unique traits to accomplish their assigned tasks. Leaders with high energy should not impose on team members. Instead, team members should be allowed the latitude needed to perform.

Reflection Questions: Energy

- Review the section on Bruce Schneider's Seven Levels of energy. Reflect on your approach at work. Which of these levels are you most closely aligned with your approach?

- What steps will you take to achieve or maintain your spot at level seven?

- Describe you daily energy cycle? What time of the day do you feel like your energy level is very high or low?

- How will you manage the following areas of your life moving forward to ensure that you are optimizing your energy levels?
  - Physical Energy
  - Spiritual Energy
  - Emotional Energy
  - Intellectual Energy

Chapter 9:
Execution

"Success doesn't necessarily come from breakthrough innovation but flawless execution."—Naveen Jain

If the journey we've been on so far could be compared to a relay race, then I take no reservations in asserting that execution is the anchoring leg of leadership.

There are many people who are gifted with great ideas and exceptional planning skills, but for some reason, they struggle to pull the trigger when it's time to execute. Watching professional athletes taking game-winning shots or businessmen making significant decisions to close a multi-million-dollar deal may appear easy, but in all honesty, not everyone is wired to handle the pressure that comes with making that move that could lead to success or failure.

Many of us criticize athletes, politicians, and leaders of organizations when we believe they were reluctant to execute their plans or promises without understanding the pressures of making decisions or taking actions that could lead to celebration or disappointment.

Since we started with sporting analogies, let me go further to say that execution is to leadership what touchdowns are to football, runs to cricket, goals to soccer, holes to golf, and baskets to basketball. In the same way, execution defines the legacy of a leader.

When faced with a myriad of challenges, ambiguity, and uncertainty, the most successful leaders are disciplined and decisive about taking the right action based on the information available to them. Suppose you've ever had the frustrating experience of working with an indecisive leader who keeps coming to you, asking for ideas or project proposals, and failing to act on any of these ideas. In that case, I am sure you understand exactly what I am saying.

It is no different from athletes with extraordinary skills, whose best games are exhibited during practice, but they will never step up and deliver the win on game day. Execution is a skill to be fine-tuned and developed over time. In this section, we will discuss some examples of leaders who have done this well. At the same time, we will look at the dark side of execution, as well as some of the strategies and disciplines we can implement to deliver on this strategy successfully.

A Leader of Execution: Winston Churchill

Looking over the course of history, numerous leaders have epitomized the key tenets of execution. My personal favorite is Sir Winston Churchill.

Sir Winston Churchill took on the reins of leadership as the 41st Prime Minister of Great Britain during one of the most tumultuous times of the country's history. He successfully led his country against the Germans during World War II.

Nazi Germany, under the leadership of Adolf Hitler, was wreaking havoc; Jews were being slaughtered or sent to concentration camps where they were treated as slaves and robbed of their human rights.

The world was in dire need of a strong and decisive leader who was willing to make tough decisions about confronting and dismantling the tyrannical empire built by Adolf Hitler. There were other leaders at the time who could have acted, but none sought to do it quite like Churchill. This void in leadership gave Hitler open range to unleash terror across Europe and, ultimately, the world.

Sir Winston Churchill had an immediate impact as he made his plans clear to confront and defeat the ambitions of a dictator who had his sights set on conquering Europe. Churchill's bold and decisive leadership of Britain during World War II gave his countrymen confidence and the world hope. He was prepared to do what it took to protect his country at all costs, even if it involved confronting allies who were on the brink of surrendering to Adolf Hitler and his regime. Churchill believed in making decisions, but he was more committed to acting above all.

His famous quote signals his stance on execution, "I never worry about action, but only worry about inaction."[lix] His philosophy on making decisions and taking action when it mattered most was not always welcomed or celebrated by his fellow politicians. But when the stakes were high, and the world found itself inches away from the domination of Adolf Hitler and his fascist beliefs, it was the leadership of a bold decision-maker, Sir Winston Churchill, which served as the light in combatting the Nazis.

With every action, there are consequences you must live with. The fear of dealing with the impact sometimes forces leaders to pass on the opportunity to make decisions or execute a given plan. Winston Churchill understood the importance of making major decisions and the consequences of those decisions. He knew full well that you can only win if you are willing to execute your plans.

In a famous speech, Churchill shared how far he was willing to go with his decision to confront and conquer Adolf Hitler, "We shall fight on the beaches, we shall fight on the landing grounds, we shall fight in the fields and in the streets, we shall fight in the hills; we shall never surrender. And even if, which I do not for a moment believe, this island or a large part of it were subjugated and starving; our Empire beyond the seas, armed and guarded by the British fleet, would carry on the struggle, until, in God's good time, the new world, with all its power and might, steps forth to the rescue and the liberation of the old."

These lines from his famous speech speak of a leader who was willing not just to cast a vision but to deliver and implement this vision through the power of execution—a willingness to support the words, ideas, plans, and vision with action.

Making tough decisions can be difficult but living with the consequences of our indecision is much worse. Your decision to execute a given plan may not be the most popular move. You may lose allies in the process, but your detractors will eventually become your cheerleaders when the fruits of your actions become evident.

Failure to Execute

For every breakthrough we've experienced in this world, whether in the domain of science, art, music, or technology, someone was willing to put their careers on the line to make that bold move and execute.

If you think about it, much of the technology and niceties we currently enjoy –our cars, homes, smart phones, smart watches - exists because someone executed on a strategy, idea, or decision. Results come as a direct result of execution. The next time you feel scared about making moves on a great plan or idea, I want you to reflect on where we would be had it not been for their bold efforts the pioneers and inventors who made all these breakthroughs possible and let that be a source of motivation for you to move forward.

Why is it that so many people find it difficult to generate sustainable growth for themselves and their organizations, while others with similar resources have shelves full of achievements? It is safe to say that inability to execute (make decisions, act, or implement strategy) significantly impacts results. When we choose not to execute, we are truly saying that we are satisfied with our current position.

Four things happen when we fail to execute as a leader:

1. Loss of momentum and relevance
2. Stagnation
3. Missed Opportunities
4. Loss of support and trust from key people

Even while acting on limited information, the leaders, coaches, executives, and athletes who have mastered the art of execution are more apt to succeed than those who set up camps in the valley of indecision. Let's be frank, there are times when leaders make the wrong moves or make a bad decision, but at the very least, they will acquire knowledge of a route that should never be taken in the future.

In a gig-like economy where things are moving at a rapid pace, we run the risk of losing momentum or relevance by our inaction or procrastination. Lost relevance can have a profound impact on you, personally and professionally.

It is crooked thinking to believe that if we hold on to what we have already accomplished for the sake of safety, without taking risks or make life-altering decisions, things will remain the same. Things will continue to change whether you make decisions or not. If you want to be a part of the change, then your best chance is to act and get comfortable with it.

One of the good things about execution is that it forces you to move from a place of comfort or complacency towards challenges and opportunities. It significantly reduces the odds of stagnation taking root in your success journey.

One example of how stagnation can be manifested at work is when people become so operationally focused that they forget the strategic context of the business. Ron Carucci suggested that one of the main factors driving execution failure is that leaders become too internally focused and neglect the strategic aspects of their roles and functions. They spend a significant amount of time resolving conflicts, reconciling budgets, and managing performance.

Though this is not always a problematic approach, Carrucci suggests that by over-indulging in the operational aspects of their business, they fail to take into consideration the competitive context of their organization[lx]. What they should do instead is to have an expanded focus that is appropriately responding to the environmental forces affecting their organization.

Stagnation and failure will not be the last enemy of those who take the time out and away from their operational job requirements to assess and act from an informed place in the entire business context.

Businesses that have failed because of no growth in recent years are on the verge of collapsing. Some leaders have avoided making tough or risky decisions in the name of job security or maintaining the status quo, only to see a shift in the entire landscape that ultimately erodes their success.

When we fail to execute, we miss opportunities. Failure to capitalize on these opportunities can land a fatal blow to our career and success, at both a team and organizational level.

In my personal observation of some of these individuals, I have discovered that they are willing to take risks and make bold decisions that may yield great results or at the very least, provide them with an opportunity to learn. In either of these cases, we can see a win-win outcome emerging.

They are never comfortable with just celebrating their victories from the good old days. In fact, most of them have difficulty celebrating because as they celebrate one achievement, they are well on their way towards the next.

Steve Harvey wrote about a concept called *The Jump*. I believe within the context of execution; this concept is quite instructive[lxi]. Today, he is celebrated as a successful actor, author, businessman, and comedian whose journey to success and prosperity required some tough decisions.

Harvey said, "If you want to be successful, you have to jump; there's no way around it. When you jump, I can assure you that your parachute will not open right away. But if you do not jump, your parachute will never open. If you're safe, you will never soar!".

In telling the story of his success journey, Steve Harvey seeks to highlight the notion of taking a leap without the assurance of a favorable outcome or safe landing. In one of the most life-changing moments of his career, Steve Harvey recounts his time waiting at the Apollo Theatre to perform for the first time on TV.

It was a tough crowd, and he watched as fellow comedians like D. L Hughley, Dwayne Johnson, Jamie Fox got booed by the audience. As he knew he was scheduled to follow, nervousness reduced him to the point of feeling nauseated. One after the other, each talented act was rejected by the audience.

He then said something that I thought was very interesting, "everyone has a turn-back moment." This is a crossroad where you have two options: to push forward and execute, or give in to the fear and pressure of losing and step back into what feels safe. Despite the wooziness in his stomach, Steve *"Jumped."* He got on stage, captivated the audience, and the rest is history. Today, we celebrate the man he has become, all because of a single act of bravery in the face of the unknown.

I'd like to compare executionary leadership with a willingness to jump. As a leader, your team looks up to you to take leaps, make moves and make decisions, while being fully aware of the fact that you run the risk of failing.

People tend to lose trust in a leader or organization when there is a failure to act. People are not inspired by a lack of action. They like to see movement and experience the positive results of change in their lives. Though they are naturally resistant to change, when they see evidence that what is being done is making a positive difference, they will consider you to be someone trustworthy.

I have mentioned before that trust is fundamental to the success of any leader. If the only thing others know about you is that you are all talk and no action, they will lose trust and confidence in your ability to lead. They feel like meetings are a waste of their time, and they won't bring their brightest ideas and perspectives to these discussions simply because they don't trust that you will act on them. They will write you off as an inept leader who does not have the credibility to implement their ideas.

Leveraging the Four Disciplines of Execution

In the book *Four Disciplines of Execution*, the authors Chris McChesney, Jim Hulling, and Sean Covey discuss the importance of sound executionary practices while providing a proven system that can help leaders build a legacy that will transcend them[lxii]. The disciplines cited below are not word-for-word what was presented, but they capture the essence of what McChesney et al. sought to unravel:

1. Prioritize 1–3 major goals that you want to accomplish.
2. Determine and take the necessary steps to realize these goals.
3. Track your progress visually.
4. Create a system or network of accountability.

We are naturally wired to win, and there's learning in whatever we do. One of the fundamental principles that serves as a driver behind our success is execution. All goals are as great as their execution. Whether they are: professional, financial, strategic, or personal—execution is what brings them to life.

Importance of Prioritization

Have you ever attended a meeting with the intention of setting some definite goals, only to leave the meeting confused and overwhelmed with the number of priorities that you decided to tackle? Nothing is wrong with having a plethora of great ideas, but if you want to maximize the use of your energy and resources, you need to focus on what is important. Having too many priorities may prevent us from being productive. We spread ourselves thin and lose the required bandwidth and productivity in multiple areas. Prioritization enhances our effectiveness and helps us determine the best places to invest our resources (time, money, and energy).

I remember a conversation with a friend during a moment of vulnerability. I shared some of the challenges I was experiencing with growing our consulting practice. As he listened to me rehearsing my problems, he shared an anecdote about someone who is very successful currently because his focus is on just one goal at a time, as he balances out the other demands that life has to offer.

We cannot invest the time and resources needed in too many goals simultaneously. That makes it impossible for us to achieve the best results because we cannot fully invest in too many priorities. I have lived it and can truly attest to the fact that the day I prioritized my goals was the day I started being productive.

When you have prioritized and narrowed your goals to one to three goals, it is time to determine the steps you need to take to achieve them—this is the fun part. What are goals without a plan of action? They are nothing but words on a page. Determining the steps and activities, then taking those steps is really the leg work of execution.

Performing an action should involve careful planning, taking into consideration some of the things we mentioned in Chapter Two (2) on Foresight that had to do with scenario planning. This is where you can develop a plan as well as contingency measures to ensure that things get done the way they should be done. Many people have great goals and strategic plans, but they miss out on identifying the steps or actions they need to take to get to the end zone.

For example, you may say I want to lose a specific amount of weight by a certain time. Until you have initiated the steps necessary to achieve this, this goal is dead. It can only be brought to life once you purchase your gym membership, adopt ta meal plan, hire a coach, and work consistently daily towards achieving this lofty idea.

By adding activities to your goals, you automatically transform them into S.M.A.R.T (Specific, Measurable, Achievable, Realistic, and Time bound) goals because you can now track and measure your results, which leads us to the next discipline.

Visibly Track your Results

Keeping your results or scoreboard in front of you reminds you of your progress and performance, which helps you create a connection between your effort, performance, and the results you seek. This process allows you to assume ownership of the results by allocating time and resources towards where it is most likely needed. We can either be encouraged or refueled by our progress, but we also run the risk of giving up too early, despite a high probability of achieving those goals in the future. We must analyze and prescribe corrective measures to move closer to our goal, while actively tracking results.

Develop a System or Network of Accountability

Accountability begins with holding yourself accountable. There must be a part of you that is willing to say, "I need to stop procrastinating; get up and go—get this done". Without this, accountability on the team level will prove difficult.

One of the fun aspects of my job as a leadership consultant has to do with culture and change management within the organizations that I work with. Team culture is one of the most challenging areas to impact; however, I do believe that one of the essential elements of impacting a team culture is accountability.

As a leader, when you are willing and open to accepting accountability from others, you have attained a level of maturity that will prove helpful along your success journey.

In our team development workshops, we have used Pat Lencioni's Five Behaviors Model to help teams work more cohesively. What we share in these sessions is that the very best way to know that your team can become a highly functional and cohesive team is when people are willing to hold each other accountable to the norms, goals, and standards of behaviors that the team has set.

Let's go back to my healthy lifestyle example. Accountability is that nudge you need from someone to stay the course. A spouse, your child, or even a friend will be able to correct you when they see you veering off course by indulging yourself in activities that would prevent you from reaching your goals.

The Executionary Leader: Michael Manley

Through research and firsthand experiences, many authors have sought, through their books, to paint a vivid picture of the impact and influence Michael Manley had through his bold and daring policies to empower and liberate his people.

Michael Norman Manley the fearless Former Prime Minister of Jamaica was one who stood for justice, equity, and a transformation for his people. In some circles he is only remembered for his mistakes but in others, he was one of the most influential leaders in the country's history.

Though he was born in affluence as the son of a former Prime Minister - Norman Washington Manley, Michael was a man with a heart for regular people. For many who suffered for decades at the hand's poverty, classism, racism, lack of national pride, lack of educational opportunities and a certain path to a substandard life, Manley was the hero who went into office and executed on some the most consequential policies that shifted the tide in favor of the poor.

Michael Manley served two terms as Prime Minister for Jamaica, 1972 to 1980 and 1989 to 1992. During this period, he implemented programs that made access to education much easier, implemented and increased the minimum living wage for the working class. He embraced democratic socialism, to the displeasure of political opponents. He then partnered with Fidel Castro for taking steps towards development for his Education and Health Ministries. His fight for equity and equality influenced him to create equal pay for women and he also took steps to remove the stigma associated with children born out of wedlock.

Probably one of the biggest and best policies executed by Manley was to provide affordable housing and land for agriculture to the working class. Under the "Project Land Lease" allowed farmers to benefit from more land space, technical support, and access to funding to expand the agricultural program.

I am sure listening to all these policy achievements by Manley one would be tempted to believe that his tenure was a very successful one. The downside of his regime is that a significant amount of capitalists and first class citizens felt alienated by Manley's messaging. They felt they were villainized by some of the statements made about rich versus poor and withdrew their capital and migrated out of the country, taking jobs and dealing a very bad blow the economic backbone of the country.

This mass-migration led to one of the worse economic downturns in the country's history. Despite his aggressive push to generate positive change on all levels for his people, he drives to execute on several fronts. Some harsh lessons came with the pace at which he executed his plans and the number of areas he attempted to execute simultaneously.

The Challenges of Execution

Execution often brings about change, and this aspect of execution can be uncomfortable for some. In fact, I will venture to say that it can lead to outright rebellion and even sabotage from those who are impacted by the change. These resulting events may even sabotage the success of the change.

The quest for consensus can be a very complicated and, sometimes, impossible challenge. Because we are dealing with so many complex human behaviors, it is very hard to pin down a perfect, people-proof approach. In fact, I will not be suggesting an ideal approach; the approach I am recommending is the one that will reduce the likelihood of sabotage.

While taking steps to execute, it is crucial for you to take into consideration the buy-in or support from others (especially those who have the most significant influence on your decision). It is also important to do this gradually, rather than abruptly, allowing others to see the benefit behind the moves you are making.

John Maxwell in one of his many talks on the *Law of Influence* talks about his experience pastoring his first church in Hillham Indiana. He joked about the size of the church and the fact that the entire church membership could probably fit in a phone booth. As John Maxwell recounts his first board meeting at Hillham church, he quite quickly discovered that he only had the title of the church pastor but a farmer by the name of Claude was really the person who everyone trusted and listened to. John Maxwell said that in his first board meeting Claude dominated the floor and everything that he suggested was supported by all present, at the end of the night Claude asked John Maxwell to pray to close the board meeting.

John Maxwell could have disregarded the power wielded by this farmer over his other members, or he could choose to leverage this power by bringing Claude along. So he met with Claude on his farm as they talked about the church and how they could work together to move things forward. This worked like magic. John shared his vision and ideas with Claude, while he listened to the Claude's feedback about the ideas shared. That was when he won the confidence of the board.

According to Maxwell, for the duration of his time at that church, he never facilitated a board meeting without calling Claude a week in advance. The church experienced exponential growth. This is proof that your ideas, projects, and potential solutions mean nothing if you fail to collaborate with the right people. Don't ever be too caught up in your idea, brilliance, and position while ignoring those who can sabotage our plans.

Strategy for Execution: Stakeholder Analysis

Having an idea of those who have power and influence over the success of our projects, ideas and decisions is made much easier with the use of a simple and straightforward tool called the *stakeholder matrix*. As illustrated in fig. 1.0, this tool helps you to identify stakeholders and manage their needs based on where they land along the spectrum of their power and interest.

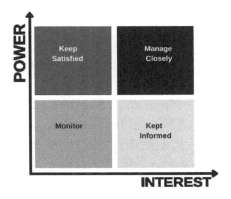

1. **Low Power and Low Interest:** Those individuals who have little power and interest in the outcome of the project or decision should be monitored

2. **High on Power and Low on Interest:** Those individuals who have a significant amount of influence but not as much influence such as government or regulator interests should be kept satisfied.

3. **High Interest and Low Power:** These stakeholders have a significant amount of interest in the outcome of the decision but have very little power to influence the decision. Some possible individuals could be employees in a company that is about to be sold. These individuals are to be kept informed.

4. **High Power and High Interest:** These individuals can completely bring your project to a screeching halt. One possible example of such a stakeholder could be an investor. These

stakeholder's needs should be closely managed.[lxiii]

People are not always willing to value the direction in which you are headed if they cannot see how the moves you make will benefit them or the organization over the long or short term. Though he was one of the most influential leaders that Jamaica has ever seen, Michael Manley lost some critical people along the way.

When asked about the criticisms he received, Prime Minister Michael Manley was quick to take ownership of the way some of the policies geared towards empowering people, were executed—that if he could have a second chance at doing it, he would have adjusted his approach, but he would not have changed anything else.

"Leaders have three fundamental responsibilities: They craft a vision, they build alignment, and they champion execution."[lxiv] It takes clarity, confidence, and awareness to execute with success. With the flawless execution of a vision, idea, or decision, we are building a legacy that could last for a lifetime. I invite you all to take the jump and unlock the amazing thrill of execution.

Reflection Questions: Execution

1. As you reflect on *The Four Disciplines of Execution* covered in the chapter, identify a project, decision or idea that you have been struggling to execute which of the following steps will you find most difficult to complete and why:

    a. Prioritize 1-3 major goals that you want to accomplish
    b. Determine and take the necessary steps to realize these goals
    c. Track your progress visually
    d. Create a system or network of accountability

2. How can the stakeholder matrix help you improve the outcome of decisions, plans and projects?

3. What is your greatest takeaway from this chapter, and how will you incorporate it as part of your leadership journey moving forward?

End Notes

i "I know I will eventually fail, and I'm still all in." Brene Brown. (2018). *Daring greatly: How the courage to be vulnerable transforms the way we live, love, parent and lead.* Audiobook

ii Success is not final, failure is not fatal, it is the courage to continue that counts... Winston Churchill Quotes. (n.d.). BrainyQuote.com. Retrieved April 15, 2022, from BrainyQuote.com Web site: https://www.brainyquote.com/quotes/winston_churchill_124653

iii "I have not failed. I've just found 10,000 ways that won't work." the commonly-quoted version of an incident recounted in F. L. Dyer and T. C. Martin *Edison: His Life and Inventions* (1910): 'I have gotten a lot of results! I know several thousand things that won't work'

iv During the American Civil War, Abraham Lincoln effectively led the Union against the Confederate charge, securing the freedom of millions of slaves ... Gienapp, William E. Abraham Lincoln and Civil War America : a Biography. New York :Oxford University Press, 2002.

v "giving up is the only sure way to fail" ...Gena Showalter The Showalter, G. (2017). *The darkest night.* HQN.

vi "Genuine foresight is not the mark of some special genius that is inexplicably bestowed on a few.... McCain, J., & Salter, M. (2008). Hard Call: Great Decisions and the *Extraordinary People Who Made Them* (1st. TRADE EDITION). Twelve.

vii "the need to be present now also means that you can perceive what the future holds and evaluating how present circumstances are preparing you to be successful when you get there Schwartz, P. (1991). *The art of the long view*. Chicago (Author-Date, 15th ed.) Schwartz, Peter. 1991. The art of the long view.

viii "Success occurs when opportunity meets preparation". Zig Ziglar Quotes." *QuotesCosmos.com*, Last modified July 31, 2021. https://www.quotescosmos.com/quotes/Zig-Ziglar-quote-6.html

ix "When the world thought that Jeff Bezos was comfortable with the numerous achievements he had amassed, he came forth with a surprise; by adding the delivery line to his operations ..." Jeff Bezos Biography. The Biography.com . https://www.biography.com/business-figure/jeff-bezos

x " Try not to get overly attached to a hypothesis just because it's yours. " Carl Sagon (1994). *The demon haunted world: Science as a candle in the dark.* New York. Random House

xi "Keep away from those who try to belittle your ambitions. Small people always do that, but only the great make you believe that you too can become great."Mark Twain Quote.goodreads.com. Retrieved March 2022. From: https://www.goodreads.com/quotes/2528-keep-away-from-people-who-try-to-belittle-your-ambitions

xii The Oxford English Dictionary, (Oxford University Press, Year of publication), s.v. "Title of Entry," URL if entry came from online source

xiii ... all successful leaders have engaged in some amount of scenario planning Schwartz, P. (1991). The art of the long view. Chicago (Author-Date, 15th ed.) Schwartz, Peter. 1991. *The art of the long view.* (p. 50)

xiv "Deliberately embrace the variety."Joe Larocci "Steps to cultivating Foresight" Seven ways to cultivate Foresight. Retrieved December 2021 from: https://www.linkedin.com/pulse/servant-leadership-7-ways-cultivate-foresight-joe-iarocci/

xv The most difficult part of my leadership is leading myself." Maxwell, John. "Becoming the Self-Aware Leader". *Podcast Title.* Podcast audio, Month Date, Year of publication. URL.

xvi Self-awareness gives you the capacity to learn from your mistakes as well as your successes. It enables you to keep growing"... Lawrence Bossidy. (n.d.). AZQuotes.com. Retrieved April 18, 2022, from AZQuotes.com Web site: https://www.azquotes.com/quote/ 830299

xvii 100% of leaders" Golman and Boyatz ". Association for Talent Development. Retrieved August 2021 from: https://www.td.org/ insights/effective-leadership-starts-with-self-awareness

xviii "We are all farmers, and whatever we sow in our garden of life will bring forth fruits. Be careful of the seeds you sow and guard your vineyard with your life. Allen, James, 1864-1912. As a Man Thinketh. Mount Vernon, N.Y. :Peter Pauper Press, 1951.

xix Some experts and psychologists have supported the fact that children inherit the dispositions and tendencies of their parents and imitate their behaviors. Saudino K. J. (2005). Behavioral genetics and child temperament. *Journal of developmental and behavioral pediatrics : JDBP, 26*(3), 214–223. https://doi.org/ 10.1097/00004703-200506000-00010

xx "Certainty is the enemy of growth and high performance. Certainty ultimately blinds you, causing you to set false and fixed limits." Burchard, Brendon, 2017. High Performance Habits: How Extraordinary People Become that Way. Hay House, Inc.

xxi "The World Heavyweight defending Champion, George Foreman, was about to defend his title against the former world champion Mohammed Ali" Oct 30, 1974 CE: *Rumble in the Jungle"*. National Geographic. Retrieved February 14, 2022.

xxii Self-Leadership is about awareness, tolerance, and not letting your own natural tendencies limit your potential Scott Belskey " Self Leadership" retrieved November 2021 from: https://www. azquotes .com/ quote/745546

xxiii The Predictive Index (2019) "The state of teams report". Retrieved May 2020 from:

xxiv "One group of people is clueless about what they would like to do " Maxwell, John C. (2012) *The 15 Invaluable Laws of Growth.* (First international trade edition). New York: Center Street

xxv "Success today requires the agility and drive to rethink, reinvigorate, react, and reinvent constantly" Bill Gates. QuoteFancy.com. Retrieved November 2021 from: https:// quotefancy.com/quote/775596/Bill-Gates-Success-today-requires-the-agility-and-drive-to-constantly-rethink"

xxvi "Leadership is influence, nothing more, nothing less". Maxwell, J. C. (1940). *21 irrefutable laws of leadership* (2nd ed.). Thomas Nelson.

xxvii "the tale of a captain aboard a British battleship, who was "making routine maneuvers on rough seas to get back to shore". David, Susan. *Emotional Agility: Get unstuck, Embrace Change and Thrive in Work and Life.* Narrated by Susan David PhD., Audible, 2016. Audiobook.

xxviii "Real integrity is doing the right thing, knowing that nobody's going to know whether you did it or not." Oprah Winfrey Quote. Passiton.com. Retrieved January 2022 from: https://www. passiton.com/inspirational-quotes/7654-real-integrity-is-doing-the-right-thing

xxix "had more spirited discussions during meetings, and secured the results they had been seeking". Lencioni, Pat. *Four Obsessions of and Extraordinary Executive.* Narrated by: Charles Stransky & Pat Lencioni. Audible, 2002. Audiobook xxx "On the personal level, clarity is achieved when someone has a deep understanding of who they are, what they hope to achieve, and how they will accomplish this" Olney, Jennifer. (2013). *Clarity brings a leader's vision to life.* Lead Change. Retrieved July 2021 from: https://leadchangegroup.com/clarity-brings-a-leaders-vision-to-life/

xxxi "It's a lack of clarity that creates chaos and frustration. Those emotions are poison to any living goal." Maraboli, Steve. (2009). Life the Truth and Being Free. Better Today Publishing.

xxxii Neal Ramon "Absence of clarity

xxxiii "Without a clear purpose, you have no foundation on which to base your decisions, allocate your time, and use your resources. Warren, R. (2002). The purpose-driven life: What on earth am I here for?. Grand Rapids, Mich: Zondervan.

xxxiv "Many people think they lack motivation when what they really lack is clarity". Clear, J. (2018). *Atomic Habits: an easy and proven way to build good habits and break bad ones*; Tiny Changes, Remarkable Results. New York: Avery, and imprint of Penguin Random House.

xxxv "Clarity...objective realities Garry Wood

xxxvi Clarity Avoiders, Clarity Pursuers, and Clarity Blind ... Martin, K. (2013). *Clarity First.* McGraw Hill.

xxxvii Moliére Quote. Goodreads.com. Retrieved February 2022 from: https://www.goodreads.com/quotes/49256-it-is-not-only-what-we-do-but-also-what

xxxviii "An arrogant person considers himself perfect. It is the chief harm of arrogance." Leo Tolstoy Quotes. (n.d.). BrainyQuote.com. Retrieved August 15, 2021, from BrainyQuote.com Web site: https://www.brainyquote.com/quotes/leo_tolstoy_802402

xxxix "we tend to think more deeply and rationally about decisions and can then come up with more creative solutions"... Unknown (2018). *Why Curiosity Matters*. The Harvard Business Review. Retrieved October 2021 from: https://hbr.org/2018/09/curiosity)

xl creating clarity, generating energy, and delivering success. Weller, Chris (2019). *6 Words that Have Transformed Leadership at Microsoft*. Neuroleadership Group. Retrieved December 2021 from https://neuroleadership.com/your-brain-at-work/microsoft-leadership-principles

xli "Think of clarity as the fuel of vision and action. If you aren't clear about the 'why and how' you will never lift your vision off the ground." Olney, J. (2013). *Clarity brings a leader's vision to life*. The Lead Change Group. Retrieved November 2021 from: https://leadchangegroup.com/clarity-brings-a-leaders-vision-to-life

xlii "I'm not the sharpest knife in the drawer, but I'm a very sharp knife, and I'm in the drawer." Mayweather, F. (2021). Floyd Mayweather : 3 Minute Interview on Success and Self-Belief. Brian Roberts YouTube Channel. Retrieved February 2022 from: https://youtu.be/y8wL9zptGZk

xliii "general self-confidence as the belief in yourself to be successful regardless of the situations, tasks, experience, or expectation"...Ruth H. Axelrod, 2017. "**Leadership and Self-Confidence**," Springer Texts in Business and Economics, in: Joan Marques & Satinder Dhiman (ed.), Leadership Today, chapter 17, pages 297-313, Springer.

xliv a feeling or consciousness of one's powers or of reliance on one's circumstances

xlv ten signs that may show that you are an insecure leader or a leader who is low on confidence.
The Leadership Gap: What Gets Between You and Your Greatness. Lolly Daskal. (New York, NY: Portfolio, 2017).

[xlvi] explains how a person can inject life and energy into their team by maintaining a healthy balance between candor and curiosity Weber. C. Conversational Capacity: The secret to building successful teams that perform when the pressure is on. New York: McGraw Hill.

[xlvii] Tyson, M. (2008). *Iron Ambition: My Life with Cus D'Amato*. P.51

[xlviii] Kay, K. & Shipman C. *The Confidence Code*. Narrated by Sandy Rustin. Audible (2014). Audiobook

[xlix] Patcher. B. (2013*). Four things you should remember about body language*. Business Etiquette. Retrieved January 2022 from: https://www.businessinsider.com/the-right-body-language-to-use-2013-8

[l] Segal, J. et al (2020). Nonverbal Communication and Body Language. Help Guide. Retrieved November 2021 from: https://www.helpguide.org/articles/relationships-communication/nonverbal-communication.htm

[li] Nick Morgan. *Power Cues*. Narrated by Stephen Bel Davies. Audible (2015). Audio Book

[lii] Carmine Gallo (2018) . Five ways to Project Confidence in Front of an Audience. Harvard Business Review Retrieved January 2022 from: https://hbr.org/2018/05/5-ways-to-project-confidence-in-front-of-an-audience

[liii] "The snap judgment people make when they witness confidence ..." Galinsky, A. and Kilduff, G. (2013). *Be seen as a Leader*. The Harvard Business Review Retrieved December 2021 from: https://hbr.org/2013/12/be-seen-as-a-leader

[liv] "catabolic and anabolic energy" Schneider, B. (2007). *Energy Leadership: Transforming your workplace and your life from the Core*. Wiley

[lv] "Leadership is influence...." Maxwell, John C. *The 21 Indispensable Qualities of a Leader: Becoming the Person That People Will Want to Follow*. Nashville, TN: T. Nelson, 1999.

[lvi] Schwartz, T. and McCarty, C. (2007). Manage Your Energy not your Time. Harvard Business Review. Retrieved January 2022 from: https://hbr.org/2007/10/manage-your-energy-not-your-time

[lvii] "You cannot lead at the highest level of love ... Craig Goeschel. *Understanding the Four Forms of Energy.* The Craig Goeschel Leadership Podcast. (Episode 57)

[lviii] Tony Robbins Quotes. (n.d.). BrainyQuote.com. Retrieved April 15, 2022, from BrainyQuote.com Web site: https://www.brainyquote.com/quotes/tony_robbins_132984

[lix] Winston Churchill Quotes. (n.d.). BrainyQuote.com. Retrieved April 15, 2022, from BrainyQuote.com Web site: https://www.brainyquote.com/quotes/winston_churchill_156874

[lx] Carucci, R. (2017). *Executives Fail to execute strategy Because they're too internally focused.* Harvard Business Review Retrieved October 2021 from: https://hbr.org/2017/11/executives-fail-to-execute-strategy-because-theyre-too-internally-focused

[lxi] Steve Harvey. *To Be Successful You have to Jump.* The Official Steve Harvey. Retrieved May 2021 from: https://youtu.be/qnmoAQakcPE

[lxii] Chicago. Covey, Sean. 2015. *4 Disciplines of Execution*. London, England: Simon & Schuster

[lxiii] Babiuch, W. and Farhar, B., 1994. *Stakeholder analysis methodologies resource book.* Golden, CO: National Renewable Energy Laboratory.

"Leadership has three responsibilities" [lxiv] Straw. J, Scullard, M and

END NOTES

Kukkomen, S. (2013) The work of Leaders. Wiley